BOYD COUNTY

APR 13 2023

PUBLIC LIBRARY

D1709112

UNITED STATES ENCYCLOPEDIAS

THE PRESIDENTS ENCYCLOPEDIA

BY DONNA B. McKINNEY

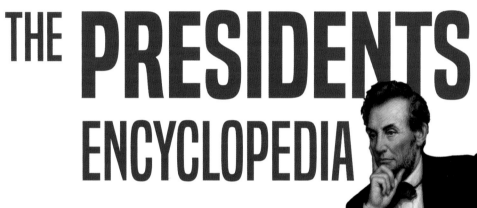

Encyclopedias

An Imprint of Abdo Reference
abdobooks.com

TABLE OF CONTENTS

In 1776, the United States of America officially announced its independence from Great Britain. People in the newly formed country now needed to determine what the new US government would look like. In 1787, delegates met in Philadelphia, Pennsylvania, to draft the US Constitution. General George Washington led the meeting. The delegates argued over a variety of issues, including what powers the head of the country should have. They feared slipping back to a government with a powerful king like the one Great Britain had.

A NEW LEADER

The delegates called this new leader the president. After long debates, the delegates finally agreed that the president would serve a four-year term. Then there would be another presidential election. The US Constitution states that the president must be a natural-born US citizen and at least 35 years old.

The United States had to fight for its independence from Great Britain in the American Revolution (1775–1783).

The president must also have been a US resident for at least 14 years.

The US president fills three main roles. First, he or she represents the country as the head of state. Second, the president chooses people to run important government departments. Third, the president is the commander in chief of the armed forces.

ELECTORAL COLLEGE

The US presidential election is an indirect election. Voters from each state choose electors to represent them in the Electoral College. The Electoral College has 538 electors. The number of electors from each state is based on the state's population. Each elector has one electoral vote. Electors are pledged to cast their votes for the presidential candidate who receives the highest number of popular votes in their state. A candidate must receive a majority of 270 Electoral College votes to become president.

Many people have served as US president. Some have led the country through difficult times, such as wars. Others signed important bills into laws. There are some presidents who are often remembered and celebrated, while others' impacts are viewed less favorably. However, each president has influenced both US and world history.

DEFINING THE PRESIDENCY

In 1789, the United States elected its first president. George Washington was one of the Founding Fathers. He helped the country gain its independence. He was a popular military leader. Washington is the only president who has been unanimously elected by the Electoral College.

Washington knew he played an important role in defining the president's responsibilities for future generations. He often said, "I walk on untrodden ground." Washington wanted the president to have enough power to govern well. But he did not want the person to rule like a king.

One of George Washington's nicknames is the "father of his country."

Martha and George
Washington married in 1759.

MARTHA WASHINGTON

Martha Washington was the first First Lady of the United States.
During the American Revolution (1775–1783), Martha often traveled.
She spent months at a time with George and his soldiers in their army
camps. While George was president, Martha was known as a gracious
hostess who was very loyal to her husband.

WASHINGTON'S ACHIEVEMENTS

One major accomplishment during Washington's presidency was the creation of the US census. This was the first population count of the American people. Washington also supported the creation of the Bill of Rights. These first ten amendments to the Constitution were added in 1791. They protect people's rights, including freedom of religion, speech, and the press.

As Washington's second term as president neared its end, people wanted him to seek a third term. But he decided to retire. Washington did not want people to view the presidency as a lifetime role. He set the standard for a two-term limit for presidents.

Although it wasn't required, Washington gave an inaugural speech after becoming president. Every US president since then has done the same.

Washington proved himself to be a capable military general before turning to politics.

QUICK FACTS

Birth and death: February 22, 1732–December 14, 1799
Wife: Martha (Dandridge Custis) Washington
Number of children: Two stepchildren
Age at inauguration: 57
Years served as president: 1789–1797
Supreme Court appointments: John Jay, James Wilson, William Cushing, John Rutledge, John Blair Jr., James Iredell, Thomas Johnson, William Paterson, Samuel Chase, Oliver Ellsworth

Key Cabinet members:
- Vice President: John Adams
- Secretary of State: John Jay, Thomas Jefferson, Edmund Randolph, Timothy Pickering
- Secretary of the Treasury: Alexander Hamilton, Oliver Wolcott Jr.
- Secretary of War: Henry Knox, Timothy Pickering, James McHenry
- Attorney General: Edmund Randolph, William Bradford, Charles Lee

ADAMS AND FRANCE

The French and British were at war when John Adams took office in 1797. France was upset that in 1794 President George Washington had signed the Jay Treaty with Great Britain. This treaty brought the United States and Great Britain closer together. As president, Adams raised a militia in case the United States had to engage in a war with France. The United States never officially went to war with France. But starting in 1798, US and French ships battled at sea until the Treaty of Mortefontaine was signed in 1800.

In 1796, John Adams narrowly won the presidency over Thomas Jefferson.

Adams inspected troops before becoming president.

ALIEN AND SEDITION ACTS

In 1798, Adams signed the Alien and Sedition Acts into law. These laws allowed the president to arrest foreigners and send them out of the country. The laws also made it a crime for people to say or print anything that harshly criticized the government. People were angry about the Alien and Sedition Acts. They saw the acts as limiting their freedoms. Many of these laws were eventually repealed.

It took eight years to build the White House.

A MOVE TO WASHINGTON, DC

In 1790, Washington, DC, became the capital of the United States. Before this time, the capital was in Philadelphia. Adams moved his family into the Executive Mansion in 1800. Later, it would be called the White House. During his second night at the White House, Adams wrote, "May none but honest and wise men ever rule under this roof." Adams ran for a second term in 1800 but lost to Thomas Jefferson.

First Lady Abigail Adams was a well-educated woman.

ABIGAIL ADAMS

First Lady Abigail Adams was a trusted adviser to her husband. She opposed slavery and supported women's education. Some people were critical of the influence she had on John's presidency. They called her Mrs. President. Abigail was also mother to the sixth president, John Quincy Adams.

QUICK FACTS

Birth and death: October 30, 1735–July 4, 1826
Wife: Abigail (Smith) Adams
Number of children: Six
Age at inauguration: 61
Years served as president: 1797–1801
Supreme Court appointments: John Marshall, Bushrod Washington, Alfred Moore

Key Cabinet members:
- Vice President: Thomas Jefferson
- Secretary of State: Timothy Pickering, John Marshall
- Secretary of the Treasury: Oliver Wolcott Jr., Samuel Dexter
- Secretary of War: James McHenry, Samuel Dexter
- Attorney General: Charles Lee

BUYING THE LOUISIANA TERRITORY

Thomas Jefferson was one of the Founding Fathers. He became president in 1801 after a heated campaign and election. The presidency was decided by Congress after a tie vote in the Electoral College.

During his first term, Jefferson bought the Louisiana Territory from France. This land covered about 827,000 square miles (2.1 million sq km) between the Rocky Mountains and the Mississippi River. The purchase of this land doubled the size of the United States. Jefferson bought it for $15 million.

People wanted to know more about the lands to the west. So in 1804, Jefferson sent out explorers. Their goal was to find a water route to the Pacific Ocean.

Thomas Jefferson is a controversial figure today. Although he made significant contributions to the country and often spoke about freedom, he enslaved hundreds of Black people.

Jefferson, *right*, was the main author of the Declaration of Independence.

A WAR IN EUROPE

Jefferson was elected to a second term in 1804. The French and British were fighting in Europe. This affected US trade there. Some British ships even attacked US ships. Jefferson wanted to punish both France and the United Kingdom for disturbing trade. So he put an embargo on US shipping. This meant US ships could not bring their goods to foreign ports. Jefferson's plan did not work well. It was very unpopular with people in the United States.

After his two terms as president, Jefferson returned to his Virginia home, Monticello. He started working on his next big project. He helped create the University of Virginia.

People today visit and tour Jefferson's Monticello estate.

The Thomas Jefferson Memorial is in Washington, DC.

QUICK FACTS

Birth and death: April 13, 1743–July 4, 1826
Wife: Martha (Wayles) Jefferson
Number of children: 12
Age at inauguration: 57
Years served as president: 1801–1809
Supreme Court appointments: William Johnson, Henry Brockholst Livingston, Thomas Todd

Key Cabinet members:
- Vice President: Aaron Burr, George Clinton
- Secretary of State: James Madison
- Secretary of the Treasury: Samuel Dexter, Albert Gallatin
- Secretary of War: Henry Dearborn
- Attorney General: Levi Lincoln, John Breckinridge, Caesar A. Rodney

THE WAR OF 1812

After becoming president in 1809, James Madison tried to keep the United States out of the conflict between France and the United Kingdom. But when the United Kingdom took control of several US ships, Madison asked Congress to declare war. This became known as the War of 1812 (1812–1814). The US Army and Navy were not strong. During the conflict, the British burned the White House and US Capitol building. But the United States fought back. In 1814, the United Kingdom and the United States signed the Treaty of Ghent, ending the war.

James Madison played a big role in writing the US Constitution. In fact, he is sometimes called the "father of the Constitution."

British troops invaded Washington, DC, in 1814 and destroyed many public buildings.

After the war, Madison set up a professional military force. He wanted to make sure the United States would be better equipped to fight any future conflicts. Madison also created a fund to help those who lost husbands and fathers in the war.

ERA OF GOOD FEELINGS

Historians give Madison credit for leading the country well through wartime. He used government resources wisely to help the US Army win several battles. Although some people loudly opposed the war, Madison held the country together. When his second term as president came to an end, the country entered a time of peace and prosperity. This period was called the Era of Good Feelings.

Despite facing some opposition to the War of 1812, Madison remained a popular president during his time.

As First Lady, Dolley Madison undertook many social obligations, including visiting the houses of all newly elected senators or representatives in Washington, DC.

QUICK FACTS

Birth and death: March 16, 1751–June 28, 1836

Wife: Dolley (Payne Todd) Madison

Number of children: One stepchild

Age at inauguration: 57

Years served as president: 1809–1817

Supreme Court appointments: Gabriel Duvall, Joseph Story

Key Cabinet members:
- Vice President: Elbridge Gerry, George Clinton
- Secretary of State: Robert Smith, James Monroe
- Secretary of the Treasury: Albert Gallatin, George W. Campbell, Alexander J. Dallas, William H. Crawford
- Secretary of War: William H. Crawford, George Graham, William Eustis, John Armstrong, James Monroe, Alexander J. Dallas
- Attorney General: Caesar A. Rodney, William Pinkney, Richard Rush

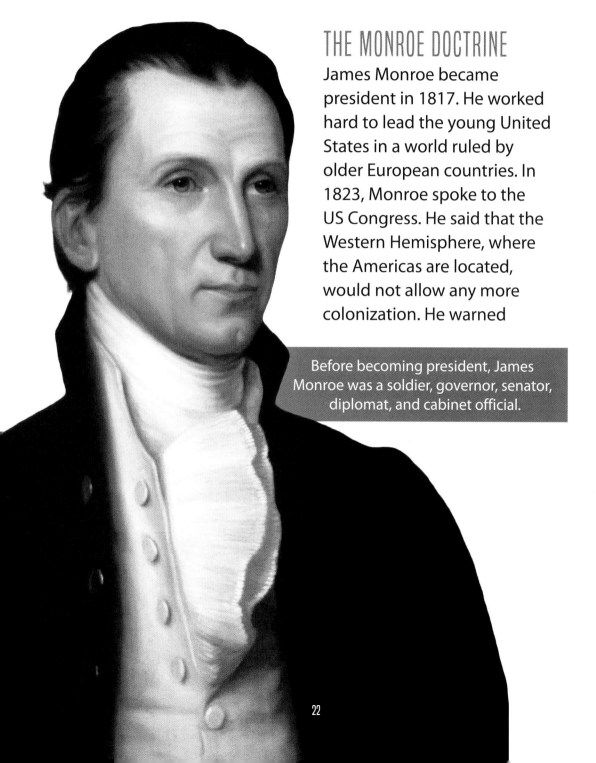

THE MONROE DOCTRINE

James Monroe became president in 1817. He worked hard to lead the young United States in a world ruled by older European countries. In 1823, Monroe spoke to the US Congress. He said that the Western Hemisphere, where the Americas are located, would not allow any more colonization. He warned

Before becoming president, James Monroe was a soldier, governor, senator, diplomat, and cabinet official.

Monroe sought the advice of his cabinet on the Monroe Doctrine.

European powers that the United States would not respond well if they tried to control any more areas in the west. This foreign policy is called the Monroe Doctrine. It is one of Monroe's most important accomplishments. It still shapes US foreign policy today.

GETTING MORE LAND

At the start of Monroe's presidency, Spain controlled the area known today as Florida. The United States wanted the land. Spain finally ceded the land in the Transcontinental Treaty of 1819.

In 1817, Missouri was a US territory. It wanted to become a state. But this caused some conflict in Congress. Some people wanted Missouri to allow slavery, while others did not. Two years later, Maine also applied for statehood. At this time, the country had 22 states. Half of them allowed slavery and the other half did not. Congress agreed to the Missouri Compromise, which allowed Missouri to become a slave state and Maine to be a free state. In 1820, Monroe signed the Missouri Compromise.

Monroe is one of three US presidents to have died on Independence Day. Both Thomas Jefferson and John Adams died on July 4, 1826.

As president, Monroe toured the country to meet with US citizens.

QUICK FACTS

Birth and death: April 28, 1758–July 4, 1831

Wife: Elizabeth (Kortright) Monroe

Number of children: Three

Age at inauguration: 58

Years served as president: 1817–1825

Supreme Court appointments: Smith Thompson

Key Cabinet members:
- Vice President: Daniel D. Tompkins
- Secretary of State: Richard Rush, John Quincy Adams
- Secretary of the Treasury: William H. Crawford
- Secretary of War: George Graham, John C. Calhoun
- Attorney General: Richard Rush, William Wirt

DECLARING A WINNER

John Quincy Adams became president in 1825 after running against Andrew Jackson. In the election, Jackson got more popular votes than Adams. But he did not win enough Electoral College votes to become president. So the US House of

John Quincy Adams was the son of John Adams, the second US president.

Louisa Adams was the first First Lady to have been born outside the United States. She was born in London, England.

Representatives decided the election. It declared Adams the winner. Adams was known to be independent and stubborn. As president, he could never rally the support he needed in Washington, DC, for his policies.

ROADS, BRIDGES, AND CANALS

Adams believed the federal government should support programs to improve life for all Americans. He proposed building a network of roads, bridges, and canals. He also suggested a national university and space observatory. But Adams lacked support in Congress and couldn't get most of his ambitious programs passed. However, Adams was able to start work on the Chesapeake and Ohio Canal. This waterway was an important route that brought coal from western Maryland to Washington, DC.

Adams ran for a second term against Jackson. Like his first election, the second one was bitter. The two candidates often spoke insultingly to each other. Adams lost his bid for reelection. Jackson won by a large margin.

After serving as president, Adams was elected to the House of Representatives for the state of Massachusetts.

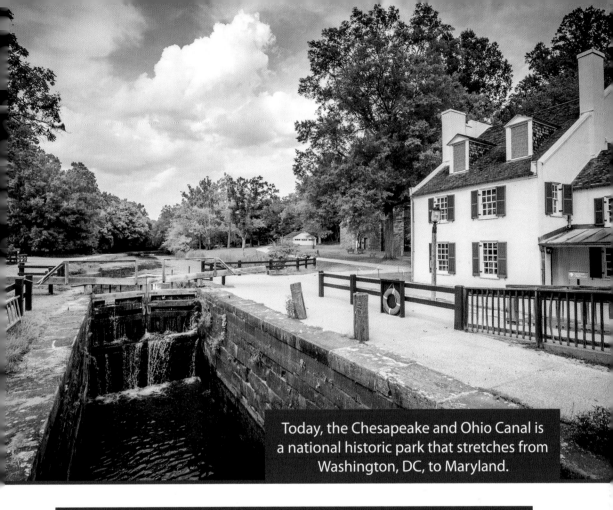

Today, the Chesapeake and Ohio Canal is a national historic park that stretches from Washington, DC, to Maryland.

QUICK FACTS

Birth and death: July 11, 1767–February 23, 1848
Wife: Louisa (Johnson) Adams
Number of children: Four
Age at inauguration: 57
Years served as president: 1825–1829
Supreme Court appointments: Robert Trimble

Key Cabinet members:
- Vice President: John C. Calhoun
- Secretary of State: Henry Clay
- Secretary of the Treasury: Richard Rush
- Secretary of War: James Barbour, Peter B. Porter
- Attorney General: William Wirt

GAINING EXPERIENCE

Andrew Jackson was a lawyer who was interested in politics. In 1796, he helped draft Tennessee's state constitution. He was also elected to the US House of Representatives that year. Jackson later served in the US Senate. These positions helped prepare Jackson for the presidency.

Andrew Jackson was the first president who had been born into poverty.

Prior to becoming president, Jackson was hailed as a hero in the War of 1812.

THE TWO-PARTY SYSTEM

Jackson was part of the Democratic-Republican Party. It was later called the Democratic Party. Jackson's victories in the 1828 and 1832 presidential elections demoralized his opponents in the National Republican Party. Around this time, a third political party formed. It was known as the Whigs, and it was made up of people who disliked Jackson. The Whig Party lasted until the mid-1850s. By 1860, the two-party system of Democrats and Republicans was in place. These are the two major political parties in the United States today. Historians view the two-party system as Jackson's legacy.

INDIAN REMOVAL ACT

In 1830, Jackson encouraged Congress to pass the Indian Removal Act. This law forced American Indians, such as the Cherokee and Creek, off their homelands in the southeastern United States. The Jackson administration forced more than 46,000 American Indians into territories west of the Mississippi River.

The journey was hazardous. For instance, between 1838 and 1839, the Cherokee people were forced to move to Oklahoma. They faced disease, hunger, and utter exhaustion. More than 4,000 people died during this journey, which is known as the Trail of Tears.

Jackson fought against the Creek Indians during the War of 1812. As president, he believed American Indians should either assimilate into US culture or leave.

The Trail of Tears route was approximately 5,045 miles (8,119 km) long.

QUICK FACTS

Birth and death: March 15, 1767–June 8, 1845

Wife: Rachel (Donelson Robards) Jackson

Number of children: One

Age at inauguration: 61

Years served as president: 1829–1837

Supreme Court appointments: Roger Brooke Taney, John McLean, Henry Baldwin, James Moore Wayne, Philip Pendleton Barbour, John Catron

Key Cabinet members:
- Vice President: John C. Calhoun, Martin Van Buren
- Secretary of State: John Forsyth, Louis McLane, Edward Livingston, Martin Van Buren
- Secretary of the Treasury: Levi Woodbury, Roger B. Taney, William J. Duane, Samuel D. Ingham, Louis McLane
- Secretary of War: Lewis Cass, Benjamin F. Butler, John H. Eaton
- Attorney General: John M. Berrien, Roger B. Taney, Benjamin F. Butler

A FINANCIAL PANIC

The country had been enjoying a prosperous time when Martin Van Buren came into the White House, but things changed quickly. Just a few months after Van Buren took office, a financial panic began. The stock market crashed. Banks and businesses failed. People lost their jobs and their land. Van Buren tried to help the country but couldn't get Congress to work with him. His popularity with the

Martin Van Buren was a lawyer before getting into politics.

US settlers and Canadian lumbermen moved into territory near the disputed US-Canada border. Tensions led to the Aroostook War (1838–1839), which was a bloodless dispute.

American people dropped. But the financial crisis wasn't the only trouble Van Buren faced during his presidency.

US-CANADA BORDER TROUBLE

The United Kingdom owned sections of Canada, and the United States and United Kingdom argued over where the US-Canada border was. A few conflicts broke out starting in 1838 between US citizens and people living in Canada. Some people urged Van Buren to go to war with the United Kingdom. Instead, Van Buren used diplomatic talks to ease the tensions. Van Buren's diplomacy strengthened the relationship between the United States and United Kingdom.

VAN BUREN AND TEXAS

During Van Buren's presidency, Texas was not yet a state. It was an independent republic that used to be part of Mexico. Some people in the United States wanted to make Texas part of the country. However, Van Buren blocked the plan to make Texas a state. He feared it would cause a war with Mexico. He also worried that Texas would become a proslavery state. Van Buren was opposed to slavery.

US settlers were drawn to Texas because of the promise of a large frontier where they could ranch and farm.

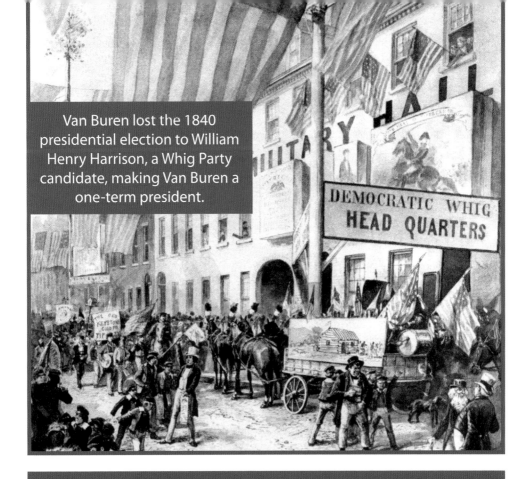

Van Buren lost the 1840 presidential election to William Henry Harrison, a Whig Party candidate, making Van Buren a one-term president.

QUICK FACTS

Birth and death: December 5, 1782–July 24, 1862
Wife: Hannah (Hoes) Van Buren
Number of children: Five
Age at inauguration: 54
Years served as president: 1837–1841
Supreme Court appointments: John McKinley, Peter Vivian Daniel

Key Cabinet members:
- Vice President: Richard M. Johnson
- Secretary of State: John Forsyth
- Secretary of the Treasury: Levi Woodbury
- Secretary of War: Joel R. Poinsett
- Attorney General: Felix Grundy, Henry D. Gilpin, Benjamin F. Butler

INAUGURATION SPEECH

William Henry Harrison served the shortest term of any US president. He died after just one month in office. Harrison gave a two-hour-long inauguration speech on March 4, 1841. It was a bitterly cold and rainy day. Harrison was outside for that entire time without a coat or hat. He contracted pneumonia and died just 32 days after he took office.

At the time, William Henry Harrison was the oldest person ever elected as president. He was 68 years old at the time of his inauguration.

An estimated 62 US soldiers died at the Battle of Tippecanoe and around 150 Shawnee Indians were killed or injured.

HARRISON AND THE MILITARY

Before he became president, Harrison was the governor of the Indiana Territory. He took lands away from American Indians. Some resisted, and in 1811, Harrison led the US Army in a battle against the Shawnee Indians at Tippecanoe River. The US forces won, and Harrison gained a military reputation. He also fought in the War of 1812 and rose to the rank of brigadier general. His military fame pushed him toward the presidency.

WHIG PARTY CANDIDATE

In 1840, Harrison ran for president as a member of the Whig Party. He was up against Martin Van Buren. The Whigs presented Harrison as a frontier fighter. They said he was a simple man in contrast to the wealthy Van Buren. However, Harrison came from a wealthy Virginia plantation family himself. He had studied the classics and history in college.

WHO'S PRESIDENT NOW?

When Harrison died, the issue of who would succeed him had to be sorted out. The Twelfth Amendment to the Constitution states that the vice president was to "act as President" when there was no president. When Harrison died, people were unsure if the vice president became president or just served until an election was held. In the end, Vice President John Tyler became president.

Harrison's 1840 campaign slogan was "Tippecanoe and Tyler too," which referenced both Harrison's military history and his running mate John Tyler.

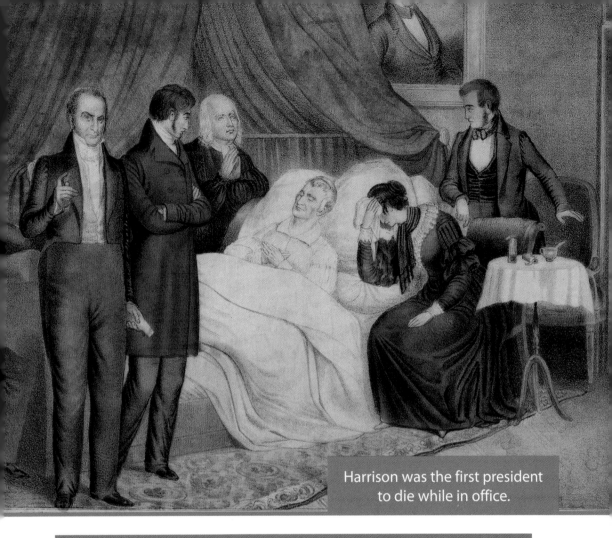

Harrison was the first president to die while in office.

QUICK FACTS

Birth and death: February 9, 1773–April 4, 1841

Wife: Anna (Tuthill Symmes) Harrison

Number of children: Ten

Age at inauguration: 68

Year served as president: 1841

Key Cabinet members:
- Vice President: John Tyler
- Secretary of State: Daniel Webster
- Secretary of the Treasury: Thomas Ewing
- Secretary of War: John Bell
- Attorney General: John J. Crittenden

SEIZING CONTROL

President William Henry Harrison died just one month after taking office. People weren't sure whether Vice President John Tyler should remain in that role and only act as president until a new election could be held, or if he should actually become president. Tyler established himself as president. He took the presidential oath of office and moved into the White House.

John Tyler had a long political history. In 1816, Virginia voters elected him to the House of Representatives. Tyler also spent time as a US senator and governor.

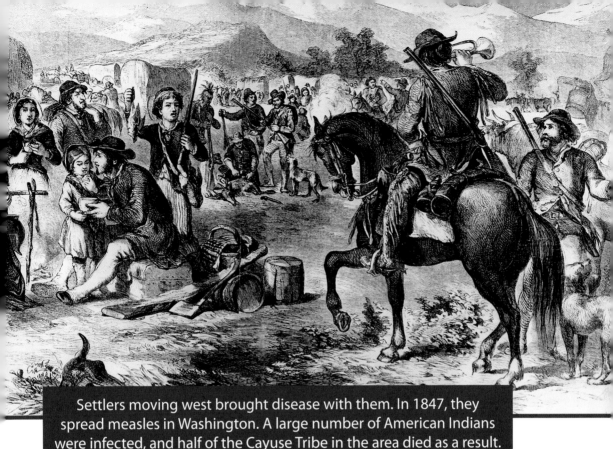

Settlers moving west brought disease with them. In 1847, they spread measles in Washington. A large number of American Indians were infected, and half of the Cayuse Tribe in the area died as a result.

VETOES, BILLS, AND TREATIES

When Tyler took office, he began to reject Whig Party programs. For example, he vetoed a bill to establish a national bank. The angry Whigs kicked him out of their party. The US House of Representatives tried to impeach Tyler. They said he abused his veto power. But the impeachment did not succeed.

In 1842, Tyler signed the Log Cabin Bill. This bill allowed settlers to claim land before it was for sale and then buy it cheaply. This bill helped Americans settle lands in the western part of the country. Tyler also backed the Webster-Ashburton Treaty. This ended a boundary dispute between Canada and the United States.

On February 19, 1846, people gathered in Austin, Texas, to celebrate Texas joining the United States. During the ceremony, the Texas flag was taken down and the US flag was raised.

THE STATE OF TEXAS

In the mid-1800s, the Republic of Texas was striving to become a US state. In 1845, three days before leaving office, Tyler signed a bill allowing Texas to enter the Union as the twenty-eighth state. This hurt US relations with Mexico, however, because Mexico saw Texas as part of its country. Despite this, some historians consider Texas's statehood to be Tyler's greatest presidential achievement.

Tyler's first wife, Letitia, had a stroke in 1842 and her health declined. Letitia was the first First Lady to die while at the White House.

QUICK FACTS

Birth and death: March 29, 1790–January 18, 1862
Wives: Letitia (Christian) Tyler (m. 1813–1842), Julia (Gardiner) Tyler (m. 1844–1862)
Number of children: 15
Age at inauguration: 51
Years served as president: 1841–1845
Supreme Court appointments: Samuel Nelson

Key Cabinet members:
- Vice President: None
- Secretary of State: Daniel Webster, Abel P. Upshur
- Secretary of the Treasury: Thomas Ewing, Walter Forward, John C. Spencer, George M. Bibb
- Secretary of War: William Wilkins, John Bell, John C. Spencer, James M. Porter
- Attorney General: John Nelson, Hugh S. Legaré, John J. Crittenden

James K. Polk was the Speaker of the House of Representatives from 1835 to 1839.

THE DARK HORSE CANDIDATE

James K. Polk was a little-known candidate when he ran for president in 1844. Historians call him the first dark horse candidate, meaning he was not expected to win but did. Polk came into office promising to be a one-term president. He did not run for reelection.

THE UNITED STATES EXPANDS

Polk was committed to expanding US lands. While he was president, the United States grew by more than 1 million square miles (2.6 million sq km).

However, his plan to get more land for the United States meant going to war with Mexico.

After the United States' victory in the Mexican-American War (1846–1848), Mexico gave up a large area of land. Today, that land makes up the states of Arizona, Utah, Nevada, California, Oregon, Idaho, and Washington. Parts of New Mexico, Wyoming, Montana, and Colorado were also included.

Around 1,500 US troops were killed in combat during the Mexican-American War, though many more died due to illnesses.

After the Mexican-American War, the Navajo people in the southwestern United States were driven off their ancestral homelands by US soldiers.

MANIFEST DESTINY

The phrase "Manifest Destiny" came to describe the way the country grew during Polk's presidency. The phrase captured the idea that the United States was appointed by God to spread westward across North America, even though American Indians already lived on those lands. Some people wanted slavery to expand west. Others did not. In addition, some people felt the expansion should only happen through peaceful ways and not by going to war.

SARAH POLK

Historians describe First Lady Sarah Polk as a dignified woman with strong religious principles. She refused to drink alcohol, dance, or attend the theater. Sarah was an educated woman and interested in politics. She edited her husband's speeches and clipped newspaper articles she thought were important for him to read. Sarah worked hard to promote her husband's career.

First Lady Sarah Polk and her husband never had any children.

QUICK FACTS

Birth and death: November 2, 1795–June 15, 1849
Wife: Sarah (Childress) Polk
Age at inauguration: 49
Years served as president: 1845–1849
Supreme Court appointments: Levi Woodbury, Robert Cooper Grier

Key Cabinet members:
- Vice President: George M. Dallas
- Secretary of State: James Buchanan
- Secretary of the Treasury: Robert J. Walker
- Secretary of War: William L. Marcy
- Attorney General: Isaac Toucey, Nathan Clifford, John Y. Mason

12TH
ZACHARY TAYLOR (1849-1850)

A MILITARY AND POLITICAL LEADER

Zachary Taylor was a military hero during the Mexican-American War. People called him "Old Rough and Ready" because he shared in the hardships of military life alongside the soldiers he commanded. That popularity as a military hero helped him win the presidency.

Taylor served only 16 months as president before he died suddenly. On July 4, 1850, he

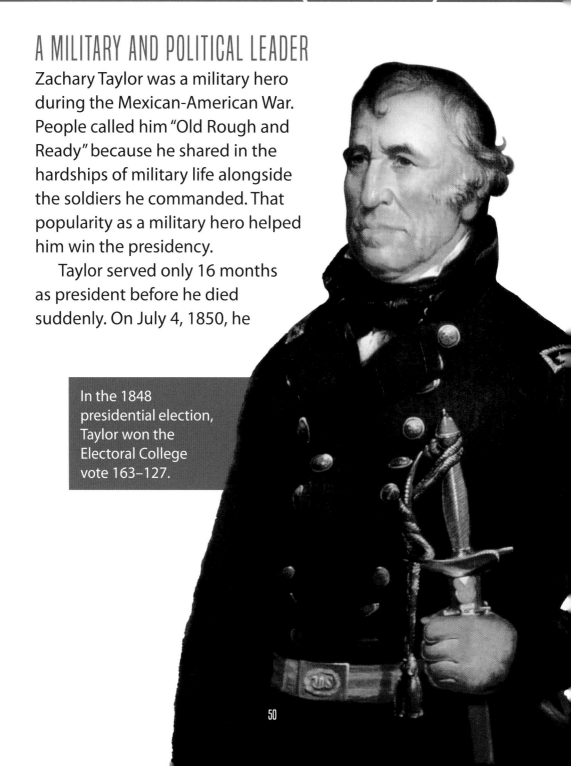

In the 1848 presidential election, Taylor won the Electoral College vote 163–127.

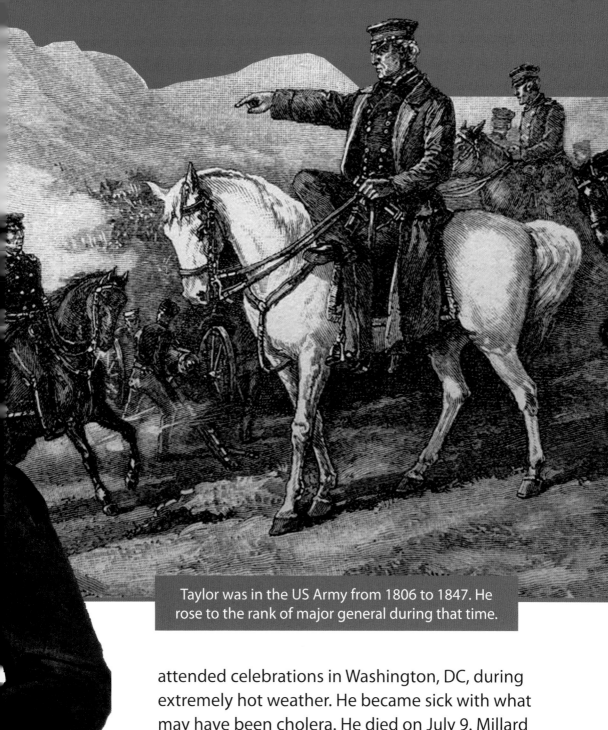

Taylor was in the US Army from 1806 to 1847. He rose to the rank of major general during that time.

attended celebrations in Washington, DC, during extremely hot weather. He became sick with what may have been cholera. He died on July 9. Millard Fillmore, his vice president, became president.

THE DEBATE OVER SLAVERY

During Taylor's short presidency, there were many arguments over slavery. The Southern states were firmly proslavery. The Northern states were against it. People disagreed on whether the national government should allow slavery to spread into new areas of the country. In particular, people argued whether slavery should be allowed in the lands that would become California, New Mexico, and Utah.

Taylor was a wealthy Southern slaveholder with lands in Louisiana, Kentucky, and Mississippi. But he worked to bring unity between the proslavery and antislavery sides. He believed in the importance of the Union and worked hard to hold the country together. When Southern leaders threatened to secede from the United States, Taylor warned he would send in the US Army to stop any rebellion. He could not find a compromise between proslavery and antislavery advocates.

During Taylor's administration, Kentucky senator Henry Clay worked to find a compromise in the slavery dispute. His proposals would later become the Compromise of 1850.

In 1848, Zachary Taylor expressed opposition to allowing new slave states into the Union.

QUICK FACTS

Birth and death: November 24, 1784–July 9, 1850
Wife: Margaret (Mackall Smith) Taylor
Number of children: Six
Age at inauguration: 64
Years served as president: 1849–1850

Key Cabinet members:
- Vice President: Millard Fillmore
- Secretary of State: John M. Clayton
- Secretary of the Treasury: William M. Meredith
- Secretary of War: George W. Crawford
- Attorney General: Reverdy Johnson

THE COMPROMISE OF 1850

Millard Fillmore was the vice president under President Zachary Taylor. When Taylor died suddenly in 1850, Fillmore assumed leadership. He inherited a country deeply divided over the issue of slavery.

When Fillmore became president, Congress was already working on a package of bills called the Compromise of 1850. The bills allowed California to become part of the United States as a free state. Utah and New Mexico would join as states where enslaving people was legal. Fillmore supported the bills. After long debates, they passed in Congress.

Millard Fillmore's support of the Fugitive Slave Act turned many Northerners against him.

Senators engaged in fierce debates over slavery.

The bills settled some questions around the expansion of slavery in the United States. But not everyone was content with the compromise. Northern members of the Whig Party were especially angry about the Fugitive Slave Act. This required Northerners to seize enslaved people who had fled the South and return them to slaveholders, even if the enslaved people were in a free state.

Fillmore was personally against the practice of slavery, but he supported the compromise anyway. This was partly due to the fear that the Southern states would secede from the Union if they didn't get what they wanted. The Compromise of 1850 kept peace between the North and South for a period of time. But the peace was short-lived. The Civil War (1861–1865) lay just ahead.

END OF THE WHIG PARTY

Fillmore was a member of the Whig Party, but it did not nominate Fillmore for reelection in 1852 because he allowed the Fugitive Slave Act to pass. The Whig Party began to fall apart in the 1850s. Members were joining the Republican Party.

Before becoming president, Fillmore served in the New York State Assembly and in the US House of Representatives.

As First Lady, Abigail Fillmore furnished the White House with three pianos and a music room. She also supplied books to the White House library.

QUICK FACTS

Birth and death: January 7, 1800–March 8, 1874
Wives: Abigail (Powers) Fillmore (m. 1826–1853), Caroline (Carmichael McIntosh) Fillmore (m. 1858–1874)
Number of children: Two
Age at inauguration: 50
Years served as president: 1850–1853
Supreme Court appointments: Benjamin Robbins Curtis

Key Cabinet members:
- Vice President: None
- Secretary of State: John M. Clayton, Daniel Webster, Edward Everett
- Secretary of the Treasury: William M. Meredith, Thomas Ewing, Thomas Corwin
- Secretary of War: George W. Crawford, Charles M. Conrad
- Attorney General: Reverdy Johnson, John J. Crittenden

TRAGEDY STRIKES

Two months before he became president, Franklin Pierce's 11-year-old son died in a train wreck. Pierce and his wife were still mourning their loss when they came to Washington, DC, for the inauguration. Pierce's speech to the American people was brief. His wife remained in their hotel room grieving. There was no inaugural ball to celebrate his presidency.

When Franklin Pierce took office, relations between Northern and Southern states were stretching to a breaking point.

Illinois senator Stephen A. Douglas presented the Kansas-Nebraska Act to Congress in 1854.

SLAVERY TENSIONS AND THE KANSAS-NEBRASKA ACT

Pierce became president at a time when tensions over the issue of slavery were rising. Pierce was ill-equipped to deal with this political environment. He tried to work for a compromise between proslavery and antislavery legislators. But the country was deeply divided.

Pierce backed the Kansas-Nebraska Act of 1854. This act allowed people in the territories of Kansas and Nebraska to choose whether to allow slavery. The act fueled tensions, and historians consider it an important event leading to the Civil War.

PIERCE'S FOREIGN POLICY

In foreign policy, Pierce secured an agreement with Mexico, called the Gadsden Purchase, that ended the border disputes in that area. Pierce also wanted to take control of Cuba—a colony that belonged to Spain. He planned to use military force if needed. However, his plan ultimately failed. The United States was criticized by European countries. Pierce's party did not nominate him to run for reelection.

Pierce served as an officer during the Mexican-American War.

Jane Pierce never wanted her husband to get involved with politics. As First Lady, she rarely attended social events.

QUICK FACTS

Birth and death: November 23, 1804–October 8, 1869
Wife: Jane (Means Appleton) Pierce
Number of children: Three
Age at inauguration: 48
Years served as president: 1853–1857
Supreme Court appointments: John Archibald Campbell

Key Cabinet members:
- Vice President: William R. D. King
- Secretary of State: William L. Marcy
- Secretary of the Treasury: James Guthrie
- Secretary of War: Jefferson Davis
- Attorney General: Caleb Cushing

JAMES BUCHANAN (1857–1861)

A BUILDUP TO WAR

James Buchanan was the last president to serve before the Civil War started. He saw many conflicts leading up to the war. One took place in the Kansas Territory between 1854 and 1859. Some people in the territory wanted slavery. Others did not. There were bitter battles between the two groups. The conflict became known as Bleeding Kansas.

Other conflicts arose during Buchanan's time in office too. In 1859, John Brown and a group of followers raided the federal armory at Harpers Ferry, Virginia. They hoped

Before becoming president, James Buchanan served in the US House of Representatives for Pennsylvania and later in the Senate. He was also President James K. Polk's secretary of state.

Dred Scott was enslaved by John Emerson, a man from Missouri. Missouri allowed slavery. But Emerson and Scott moved to a state and later a territory that did not allow slavery. Scott used these moves as a foundation for his lawsuit.

to start a revolution and free enslaved people. However, troops arrived and fought Brown and his followers. Brown was taken prisoner and found guilty of treason. He was hanged on December 2. This event further divided the North and the South.

THE DRED SCOTT DECISION

During his inaugural speech on March 4, 1857, Buchanan referred to slavery in the territories as a matter of little importance. That's because he believed the Supreme Court would soon settle the issue. Just two days later, the Supreme

Court reached a decision on the case *Dred Scott v. Sandford*. In this case, Dred Scott, an enslaved person, sued for his freedom and lost. Southerners celebrated the decision. Northerners were furious. Tensions over slavery rose.

SOUTHERN STATES SECEDE

With people on both sides of the slavery issue calling for action, a strong president was needed. A leader who could manage the extreme voices might have kept the country from moving toward war. Historians say that Buchanan did not take a firm position for or against slavery. After Abraham Lincoln won the 1860 presidential election, several Southern states broke away from the United States in the winter of 1860–1861. Buchanan did not stop them.

Southern states that left the Union set up their own government and military.

Buchanan is one of two presidents born in Pennsylvania.

QUICK FACTS

Birth and death: April 23, 1791–June 1, 1868

Age at inauguration: 65

Years served as president: 1857–1861

Supreme Court appointments: Nathan Clifford

Key Cabinet members:
- Vice President: John C. Breckinridge

- Secretary of State: Lewis Cass, Jeremiah S. Black
- Secretary of the Treasury: Howell Cobb, Philip F. Thomas, John A. Dix
- Secretary of War: John B. Floyd, Joseph Holt
- Attorney General: Jeremiah S. Black, Edwin M. Stanton

A REMARKABLE PRESIDENT

Historians praise Abraham Lincoln for his leadership, political skills, and integrity. Lincoln did not support slavery. When he was elected president in 1860, seven proslavery Southern states decided to split off from the United States. Four more states soon joined them. These states formed the Confederate States of America. When Lincoln became president in 1861, he inherited a deeply divided nation.

In his inauguration speech, Abraham Lincoln told the Southern states his government would not allow them to break apart the country.

66

The Battle of Gettysburg occurred in July 1863. It was a turning point in the war in favor of the Union.

THE CIVIL WAR

In South Carolina, Fort Sumter was under Union control. The Confederacy demanded that Union troops abandon the fort. The troops refused, and the Confederacy attacked the fort on April 12, 1861. The Civil War had begun.

When Fort Sumter was attacked, Lincoln raised the Union Army. The Civil War lasted four years. More than 600,000 Americans had died by the time Lincoln and the Union Army claimed victory.

EMANCIPATION PROCLAMATION

On New Year's Day in 1863, Lincoln issued the Emancipation Proclamation. This gave some enslaved people their freedom. Historians consider Lincoln's proclamation to be the most revolutionary action a US president had ever taken. But the war was still raging. The Union Army needed to win to ensure freedom for all enslaved people. However, Lincoln's proclamation set the country on a path toward greater freedoms for everyone.

Lincoln won reelection to a second term and was working toward an end to the fighting. Less than a week after the Confederate Army surrendered, Lincoln was assassinated by John Wilkes Booth, who was proslavery and disliked Lincoln. The president's legacy, however, lived on. Lincoln had accomplished his goal of preserving the Union.

Lincoln consulted his cabinet members on the Emancipation Proclamation.

Lincoln's funeral procession started in Washington, DC, and ended in Illinois. Approximately 25 million people paid their respects to Lincoln during this time.

QUICK FACTS

Birth and death: February 12, 1809–April 15, 1865
Wife: Mary (Todd) Lincoln
Number of children: Four
Age at inauguration: 52
Years served as president: 1861–1865
Supreme Court appointments: Noah Haynes Swayne, Samuel Freeman Miller, David Davis, Stephen Johnson Field, Salmon Portland Chase

Key Cabinet members:
- Vice President: Hannibal Hamlin, Andrew Johnson
- Secretary of State: William H. Seward
- Secretary of the Treasury: Salmon P. Chase, William P. Fessenden, Hugh McCulloch
- Secretary of War: Simon Cameron, Edwin M. Stanton
- Attorney General: Edward Bates, James Speed

17TH
ANDREW JOHNSON (1865–1869)

RECONSTRUCTION

Andrew Johnson was Abraham Lincoln's vice president. When Lincoln was assassinated in 1865, Johnson became president. The Civil War had ended, but there were still troubles in the South. For instance, some white people did not want newly freed African Americans to have rights equal to theirs. They tried to keep African Americans from doing many things, such as voting. Johnson and Congress tried to work together to rebuild the country after the Civil War. This period is known as Reconstruction.

BRINGING SOUTHERN STATES INTO THE UNION

Johnson worked hard to bring the Southern states back into the Union. He pardoned Confederate leaders who pledged themselves to the United States. Then he let them form new state governments. The states ratified the Thirteenth Amendment in December 1865, abolishing slavery. Some Southern states passed Black Codes in 1865 and 1866 in response. These codes severely restricted the rights of African

Andrew Johnson was the first president to be impeached.

The purpose of the Black Codes was to strip African Americans of their freedoms and force them into low-wage work.

Americans. For example, African Americans could not rent or own farms. They could not attend schools with white children. These codes were a slide back toward slavery.

CONFLICTS WITH CONGRESS

Johnson sometimes clashed with members of Congress. They didn't always agree on how Reconstruction in the South should go. Some Republicans wanted to pass bills that would protect African Americans from Black Codes, but Johnson used his presidential veto power to block them. He thought the legislation was an overreach of the federal government's powers, and that the federal government shouldn't be so involved in state affairs. Congress overruled some of Johnson's vetoes, such as the Civil Rights Bill of 1866. This law gave citizenship to most men who were born in the country. Congress then went a step further and proposed new Constitutional Amendments. The Fourteenth Amendment was ratified in 1868. It gave African Americans US citizenship and equal protection under the law. The Fifteenth Amendment was proposed in 1869 and ratified in 1870. This amendment gave African American men voting rights. During this time, the US House of Representatives voted to impeach Johnson. They wanted to remove him from office. They said he had broken a law by dismissing a government official without the approval of Congress. However, the Senate ultimately decided to keep Johnson in office.

School segregation in the United States lasted for decades. African American students did not get the same educational opportunities as white students.

One thousand people attended each day of Johnson's impeachment trial in 1868.

QUICK FACTS

Birth and death: December 29, 1808–July 31, 1875

Wife: Eliza (McCardle) Johnson

Number of children: Five

Age at inauguration: 56

Years served as president: 1865–1869

Key Cabinet members:
- Vice President: None
- Secretary of State: William H. Seward
- Secretary of the Treasury: Hugh McCulloch
- Secretary of War: Edwin M. Stanton, Ulysses S. Grant, John M. Schofield
- Attorney General: James Speed, Henry Stanbery, William M. Evarts

A MILITARY LEADER TURNED PRESIDENT

During the Civil War, Ulysses S. Grant commanded the Union Army to victory against the Confederate Army. Grant was a strong military leader. He inspired the men fighting for him. Grant decided to run for president in 1868. He wanted to make sure that the United States remained strong. He wanted to protect the rights of African Americans. Grant easily won the presidential election.

Ulysses S. Grant had a reputation for being an honorable man, but there were several scandals during his presidency.

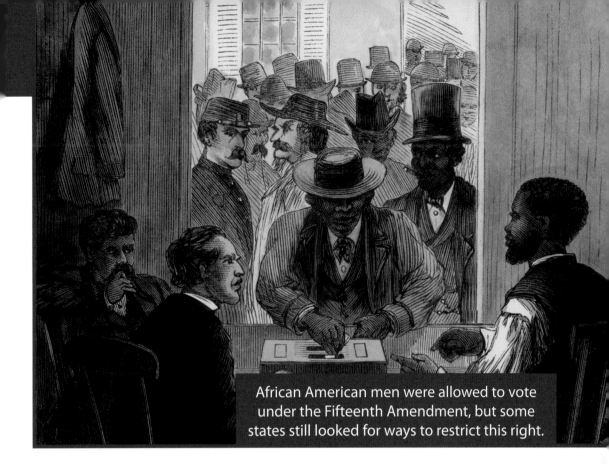

African American men were allowed to vote under the Fifteenth Amendment, but some states still looked for ways to restrict this right.

AFRICAN AMERICAN RIGHTS

Racism was a problem throughout the country, in both the South and the North. White Northerners generally favored ending slavery. But that did not necessarily mean they thought African Americans were their equals. Federal laws had to be passed to protect African Americans throughout the country. During his presidency, Grant supported the ratification of the Fifteenth Amendment that gave African American men the right to vote.

Grant also signed the Ku Klux Klan Act in 1871. Members of this terrorist group attacked African Americans. The act tried to stop the rise of the Klan in the South.

A GOLDEN CONTROVERSY

Grant's presidency faced scandals. One scandal began in 1869. At that time, gold was very valuable. Two men in New York wanted to manipulate Grant into not selling any of the US government's gold. That way, their gold would be worth even more. Grant found out what was happening. He quickly sold a large amount of the government's gold. The price of gold crashed, and people lost their savings. They were upset with Grant over his actions.

The Ku Klux Klan Act did not dismantle the group. The Klan was still active into the 2000s and was still considered a terrorist organization.

Julia Grant visited her husband as much as she could while he was fighting in the Civil War.

QUICK FACTS

Birth and death: April 27, 1822–July 23, 1885
Wife: Julia (Boggs Dent) Grant
Number of children: Four
Age at inauguration: 46
Years served as president: 1869–1877
Supreme Court appointments: William Strong, Joseph P. Bradley, Ward Hunt, Morrison Remick Waite
Key Cabinet members:
- Vice President: Schuyler Colfax, Henry Wilson
- Secretary of State: Elihu B. Washburne, Hamilton Fish
- Secretary of the Treasury: George S. Boutwell, William A. Richardson, Benjamin H. Bristow, Lot M. Morrill
- Secretary of War: John A. Rawlins, William T. Sherman, William W. Belknap, Alphonso Taft, James D. Cameron
- Attorney General: Ebenezer R. Hoar, Amos T. Akerman, George H. Williams, Edwards Pierrepont, Alphonso Taft

A DISPUTED ELECTION

Rutherford B. Hayes assumed the presidency in 1877 after a controversial election. The other candidate, Samuel Tilden, got around 250,000 more popular votes. Yet the electoral votes favored Hayes. In some states, the electoral votes were disputed. It took months for Congress to decide the election in favor of Hayes.

Rutherford B. Hayes fought in the Civil War before getting into politics.

THE END OF RECONSTRUCTION

After the Civil War, federal troops had been sent to some Southern states to maintain order. In April 1877, Hayes withdrew the US Army from Louisiana and South Carolina. When the army left, Reconstruction ended.

As president, Hayes fought political corruption. He also started civil service reform programs. These programs tested potential workers so the best people would be selected for the jobs. He also stopped the practice of removing American Indians from their homelands.

Congress declared Hayes as the president on March 2, 1877—two days before the inauguration.

Hayes's government spent millions of dollars to support American Indians who lived on unsuitable reservations.

THE GOVERNMENT'S GOLD SUPPLY

The economy had been struggling since before Hayes became president. In response, he built up the government's supply of gold. Hayes also allowed the government to buy back the special currency issued during the Civil War and return to currency backed by gold or silver. These actions helped restore the economy. People and businesses became more prosperous.

First Lady Lucy Hayes was a big supporter of the temperance movement, which aimed to prohibit alcohol.

QUICK FACTS

Birth and death: October 4, 1822–January 17, 1893
Wife: Lucy (Ware Webb) Hayes
Number of children: Eight
Age at inauguration: 54
Years served as president: 1877–1881
Supreme Court appointments: John Marshall Harlan, William Burnham Woods

Key Cabinet members:
- Vice President: William A. Wheeler
- Secretary of State: William M. Evarts
- Secretary of the Treasury: John Sherman
- Secretary of War: George W. McCrary, Alexander Ramsey
- Attorney General: Charles Devens

FRONT PORCH CAMPAIGN

James A. Garfield was a Union military officer during the Civil War. Then he was elected to Congress for the state of Ohio. Garfield served for 18 years in the US House of Representatives before becoming president in 1881.

While running for president, Garfield's campaign was called the "Front Porch Campaign." Garfield gave speeches from the porch of his house in Ohio. He won the election. In his inauguration speech, Garfield spoke of his support for voting rights and education for African Americans, especially in the Southern states. Garfield did not live long enough to make progress on these issues, however.

James A. Garfield grew up in poverty but rose to become a lawyer and politician.

Garfield watches the inaugural parade thrown in his honor on March 4, 1881.

GARFIELD ASSASSINATED

Garfield had been president just four months when Charles Julius Guiteau shot him on July 2, 1881. Guiteau was a disgruntled man who had not gotten the job he wanted in Garfield's administration. Doctors could not remove the bullet, and Garfield never recovered from the wound. On September 19, he died of blood poisoning.

TAKING A STAND

Garfield's time as president was very short. But while in office, he refused to be manipulated by politicians. He did this by taking a stand against an influential New York politician named Roscoe Conkling. Conkling had a reputation for rewarding his friends with government jobs. Conkling supported Garfield's campaign for the presidency. He expected Garfield to reward him by giving government jobs to Conkling's friends. Garfield refused to do this. He wanted government jobs to be handled fairly.

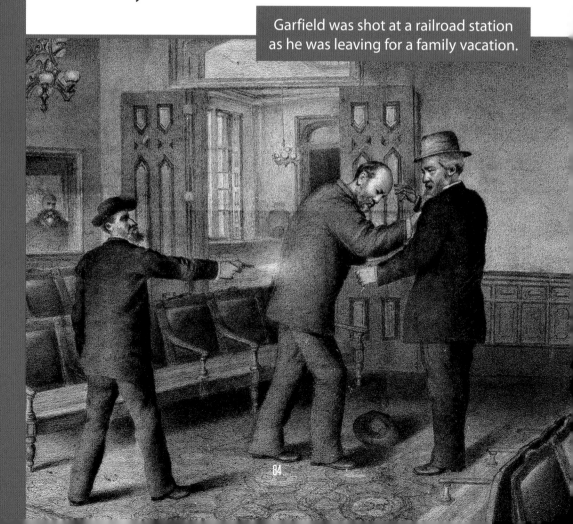

Garfield was shot at a railroad station as he was leaving for a family vacation.

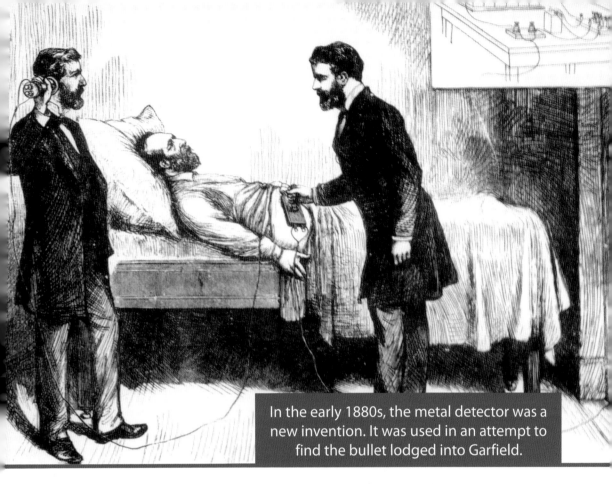

In the early 1880s, the metal detector was a new invention. It was used in an attempt to find the bullet lodged into Garfield.

QUICK FACTS

Birth and death: November 19, 1831–September 19, 1881

Wife: Lucretia (Rudolph) Garfield

Number of children: Seven

Age at inauguration: 49

Year served as president: 1881

Supreme Court appointments: Stanley Matthews

Key Cabinet members:
- Vice President: Chester A. Arthur
- Secretary of State: James G. Blaine
- Secretary of the Treasury: William Windom
- Secretary of War: Robert Todd Lincoln
- Attorney General: Isaac Wayne MacVeagh

THE CHINESE EXCLUSION ACT

Chester A. Arthur was vice president when President James A. Garfield was assassinated in 1881. Arthur then assumed office. A year later, he signed the Chinese Exclusion Act. This law stopped Chinese immigration to the United States for ten years. It was the first federal law to stop immigration of a specific nationality of people.

Before getting into politics, Chester A. Arthur was a lawyer.

Under the Chinese Exclusion Act, both state and federal courts were prohibited from giving Chinese immigrants citizenship.

Many Chinese laborers worked in California. Some white Americans viewed Chinese immigrants as dangerous people who were taking away their jobs. Historians think the Chinese Exclusion Act arose out of those racist, anti-Chinese feelings. With this law, the United States shifted away from being a country where almost all immigrants were welcome.

CIVIL SERVICE REFORM

As president, Arthur worked to reform hiring practices for federal government jobs. Politicians sometimes gave jobs to their friends regardless of whether these people were qualified for the positions. Arthur supported the Pendleton Civil Service Act of 1883. This act created the Civil Service Commission. It established the system for federal employees to be hired based on their skills rather than as a reward for supporting political candidates. Arthur's actions angered some of his old political friends.

Arthur did not put a lot of effort into his reelection in 1884. Two years previously, he had been diagnosed with a fatal kidney disease. He never told the public about it. Arthur also faced opposition from his old friends, who were still upset about the Pendleton Civil Service Act. Arthur didn't get his party's presidential nomination that year. He served out the remainder of his term and then left office.

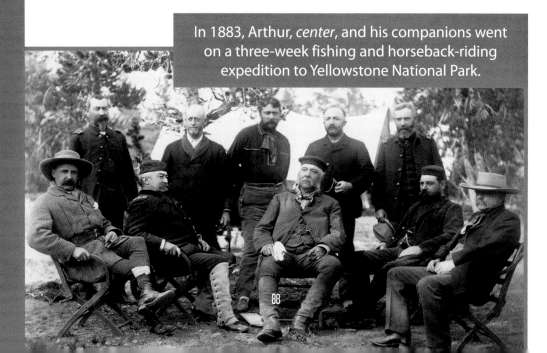

In 1883, Arthur, *center*, and his companions went on a three-week fishing and horseback-riding expedition to Yellowstone National Park.

Arthur's wife, Ellen, never made it to the White House. She passed away in 1880 of pneumonia.

QUICK FACTS

Birth and death: October 5, 1829–November 18, 1886
Wife: Ellen (Lewis Herndon) Arthur
Number of children: Three
Age at inauguration: 51
Years served as president: 1881–1885
Supreme Court appointments: Horace Gray, Samuel Blatchford
Key Cabinet members:
- Vice President: None
- Secretary of State: James G. Blaine, Frederick T. Frelinghuysen
- Secretary of the Treasury: William Windom, Charles Folger, Walter Q. Gresham, Hugh McCulloch
- Secretary of War: Robert Todd Lincoln
- Attorney General: Isaac Wayne MacVeagh, Benjamin H. Brewster

PRESIDENTIAL POWERS

Grover Cleveland is the only president to serve two terms that were not in a row. Cleveland was president from 1885 to 1889. He served again from 1893 to 1897.

Cleveland did not seem to come into office with any grand plans or agenda.

Grover Cleveland entered politics in 1881 when he became the mayor of Buffalo, New York.

FRANCES CLEVELAND

Grover Cleveland was not married when he first took office in 1885. One year later, however, he became the first president to marry during his term. He married Frances Folsom on June 2, 1886. Frances was 21 years old and college educated. She spoke French and German, played the piano, and enjoyed photography. The US public loved her, and the First Lady became quite a celebrity.

Cleveland and Frances Folsom got married in the White House—the only president and First Lady to do so.

Historians say that he viewed himself more as a watchdog of Congress. During his presidency, Cleveland made the executive branch more powerful. One way he achieved this was through the use of the presidential veto to stop any laws he did not want passed. Cleveland vetoed 414 bills during his first term as president. This is more than twice the number of vetoes used by all the presidents before him.

Cleveland showed his presidential power in other ways too. A president has the ability to send federal troops to help in a situation like a strike or a riot. In 1894, Pullman train car workers went on strike in Chicago, Illinois. Their company had cut their already low wages. The strike stalled railroad travel and mail service in many parts of the country. Cleveland sent in federal troops to stop the strike. Business leaders cheered Cleveland's decision to intervene. But laborers, who supported the Pullman train car workers' fight for better wages, strongly criticized the move.

DAWES GENERAL ALLOTMENT ACT

While Cleveland was president, there was a push to take away American Indians' sense of self and culture. For years the US government had forced American Indians off their traditional lands and onto reservations. From the 1870s to 1900s, the US government decided it wanted to break up the reservations and give the land to individual American Indians, rather than allowing many members of the tribes or nations to hold the land. It hoped these individuals would take up the white person's way of farming the land. Overall, the

Federal laws paved the way for westward expansion.

Starting in the late 1860s, hundreds of thousands of American Indian children were taken from their families and forced into boarding schools. The goal of these often abusive schools was to strip American Indians of their ways of life.

government's plan was to make American Indians leave their ways of life behind and adopt white culture.

It was in this environment that Cleveland signed the Dawes General Allotment Act in 1887. The act allowed the president to redistribute reservation lands to individual American Indians. But the land given to people was not suitable for farming. In fact, many areas were desert-like. In addition, some American Indians did not want to farm or work in agriculture. Those who were interested could rarely afford the materials needed to start a farm, such as seeds, animals, and tools. Any extra land was sold to non-Native people. This made American Indian reservations even smaller.

ECONOMIC DEPRESSION

In 1893, the country suffered a severe economic depression. Unemployment rose to 18 percent. Banks closed. Farms and businesses failed. Some unemployed people went to Washington, DC. They asked the government for help. They wanted Cleveland to organize public works programs so they could get jobs. But Cleveland didn't think the federal government should get involved in works programs. Ultimately, Cleveland could not bring the country out of the financial depression.

In 1894, unemployed men marched from Ohio to Washington, DC. They were called Coxey's Army after the businessman who led them.

In 1892, Cleveland easily beat President Benjamin Harrison in the presidential election.

QUICK FACTS

Birth and death: March 18, 1837–June 24, 1908
Wife: Frances (Folsom) Cleveland
Number of children: Five
Age at inaugurations: 47 and 55
Years served as president: 1885–1889 and 1893–1897
Supreme Court appointments: Lucius Quintus C. Lamar, Melville Weston Fuller, Edward White, Rufus W. Peckham
Key Cabinet members:
- Vice President: Thomas A. Hendricks, Adlai E. Stevenson
- Secretary of State: Thomas F. Bayard, Walter Q. Gresham, Richard Olney
- Secretary of the Treasury: Daniel Manning, Charles S. Fairchild, John Carlisle
- Secretary of War: William C. Endicott, Daniel S. Lamont
- Attorney General: Augustus H. Garland, Richard Olney, Judson Harmon

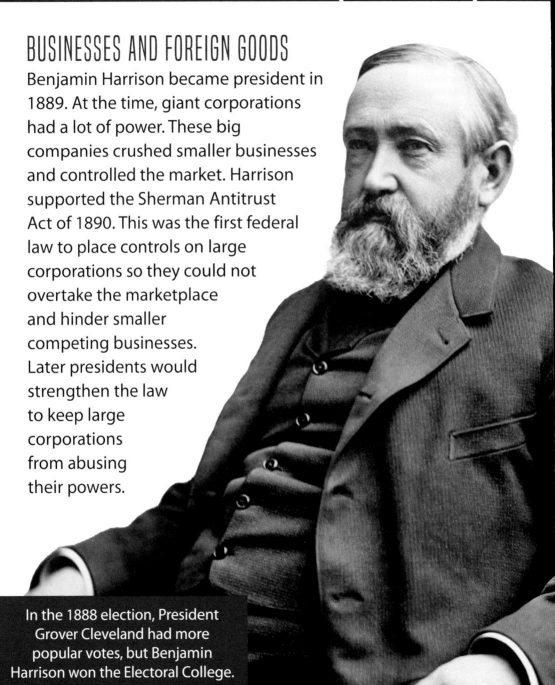

23RD
BENJAMIN HARRISON (1889–1893)

BUSINESSES AND FOREIGN GOODS

Benjamin Harrison became president in 1889. At the time, giant corporations had a lot of power. These big companies crushed smaller businesses and controlled the market. Harrison supported the Sherman Antitrust Act of 1890. This was the first federal law to place controls on large corporations so they could not overtake the marketplace and hinder smaller competing businesses. Later presidents would strengthen the law to keep large corporations from abusing their powers.

In the 1888 election, President Grover Cleveland had more popular votes, but Benjamin Harrison won the Electoral College.

Prior to his presidency, Harrison was a Union officer and later a brevet brigadier general in the Civil War.

Harrison also supported the McKinley Tariff Act of 1890. This put a tariff, or tax, on foreign goods. The goal was to protect US products and encourage Americans to buy things made in the United States. This tariff was not popular because it caused prices to rise.

BILLION-DOLLAR CONGRESS AND CIVIL RIGHTS

The federal budget grew tremendously during Harrison's term. Critics called this budget increase the "billion-dollar Congress." Harrison backed the lavish spending bills put forth by the legislative branch. With Congress spending so much money, the prosperity the country was experiencing began to disappear. This spending by Congress was a cause of the US economy's collapse in 1893.

Harrison fought hard for civil rights laws. These laws were designed to ensure that African Americans could freely vote, but they did not pass in Congress. However, Harrison's work to strengthen voting rights laid a foundation for later civil rights laws that would pass.

In 1889, Harrison signed a bill that opened land in Oklahoma Territory to white settlement. This land had previously been held for American Indians. On April 22, thousands of settlers raced across the border to stake claims.

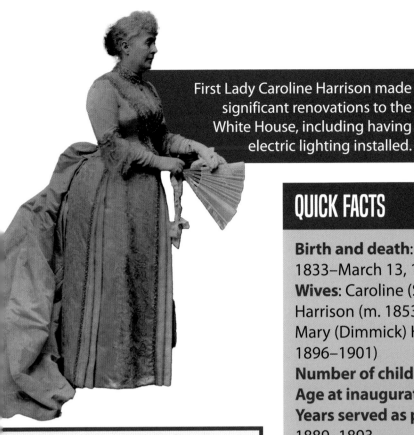

First Lady Caroline Harrison made significant renovations to the White House, including having electric lighting installed.

QUICK FACTS

Birth and death: August 20, 1833–March 13, 1901
Wives: Caroline (Scott) Harrison (m. 1853–1892), Mary (Dimmick) Harrison (m. 1896–1901)
Number of children: Three
Age at inauguration: 55
Years served as president: 1889–1893
Supreme Court appointments: David Josiah Brewer, Henry Billings Brown, George Shiras Jr., Howell Edmunds Jackson
Key Cabinet members:
- Vice President: Levi P. Morton
- Secretary of State: James Blaine, John W. Foster
- Secretary of the Treasury: William Windom, Charles Foster
- Secretary of War: Redfield Proctor, Stephen B. Elkins
- Attorney General: William H. Miller

SPANISH-AMERICAN WAR

William McKinley became president in 1897. A year later, the United States got involved in the Spanish-American War (1898). During this time, Cuba was fighting for its freedom from Spain. McKinley first worked to find diplomatic solutions. However, US troops eventually joined the fight, helping Cuba gain its freedom. The United States had business ties in Cuba and wanted to protect US investments. The war ended three and a half months later with the Treaty of Paris. With this treaty, the United States gained control of Puerto Rico, Guam, and the Philippines. McKinley's influence grew due to his handling of the Spanish-American War and the treaty that followed.

William McKinley was a teacher, a soldier, and a lawyer before entering politics at age 34.

In the Battle of Manila Bay during the Spanish-American War, the US Navy defeated the Spanish Pacific fleet. It helped solidify the United States' position as a naval power.

OPEN DOOR POLICY

The United States wanted to keep good trade relations with China and to protect its ports so that all countries could have equal access to trade there. To do this, McKinley signed the Open Door Policy. This was a series of documents the United States issued between 1899 and 1900. This policy protected US trading rights in China. It also showed US support for a free and independent China not colonized by other nations. Historians consider McKinley's Open Door Policy to be one of his most important policies. It helped to keep China an independent country and protected open trade between China and other countries.

BACKED BY GOLD

In domestic affairs, questions arose about the US currency. Some people pushed for a bimetal standard, where silver and gold backed US currency. With the Gold Standard Act of 1900, McKinley placed US money on the gold standard. All US money was backed by gold. This act prevented the country from printing too much paper money and running out of gold. McKinley was elected to a second term in 1900. But in September 1901, he was shot by an assassin. McKinley died eight days later.

McKinley's vice president, Theodore Roosevelt, *right*, had the job for less than a year before McKinley was assassinated.

McKinley had a funeral procession in Washington, DC, where people came out to pay their respects.

QUICK FACTS

Birth and death: January 29, 1843–September 14, 1901
Wife: Ida (Saxton) McKinley
Number of children: Two
Age at inauguration: 54
Years served as president: 1897–1901
Supreme Court appointments: Joseph McKenna
Key Cabinet members:
- Vice President: Garret A. Hobart, Theodore Roosevelt
- Secretary of State: John Sherman, William Day, John M. Hay
- Secretary of the Treasury: Lyman J. Gage
- Secretary of War: Russell Alger, Elihu Root
- Attorney General: Joseph McKenna, John W. Griggs, Philander C. Knox

SOCIAL AND ECONOMIC CHANGE

When President William McKinley was assassinated in 1901, Vice President Theodore Roosevelt became president. Roosevelt used his presidential powers to push for social and economic justice. He worked to protect the environment. He also took a proactive role in foreign policy.

At the time, Theodore Roosevelt was the youngest president in US history at age 42.

Roosevelt greatly respected nature and wanted to protect it. In addition to establishing five national parks, Roosevelt created 150 national forests, four game preserves, and dozens of bird reserves.

CONSERVATION AND CIVIL RIGHTS

Roosevelt had a significant impact when it came to land conservation. During his presidency, Roosevelt created five national parks. He banned mining in Arizona's Grand Canyon. Roosevelt also worked to create projects that allowed farming in desert areas. In addition, he strove to establish national forests and bird refuges.

Roosevelt supported projects to help less-wealthy citizens, such as some single mothers with children. He also supported the fight for women's right to vote. Yet when it came to racial issues, Roosevelt reflected the common attitudes of the time. Roosevelt wrongly believed that African Americans were not equal to white people.

PANAMA CANAL

When it came to foreign affairs, Roosevelt worked toward peaceful agreements. He mediated peace negotiations when fighting started between Russia and Japan in 1904. But he made it clear he would use military force if needed. Roosevelt built the US Navy to become one of the world's biggest. Then he sent the US fleet on a world tour to display the United States' naval power.

Roosevelt's biggest foreign policy success was the creation of the Panama Canal. Roosevelt oversaw the start of this major project. This important man-made waterway connected the Pacific and Atlantic oceans, allowing countries to ship goods quickly and cheaply between the Pacific and Atlantic coasts. It made the trip from San Francisco, California, to New York 8,000 miles (12,875 km) shorter when traveling by water.

The US naval force sent out on Roosevelt's orders included 16 battleships. They were on tour for 14 months and were called the "great white fleet."

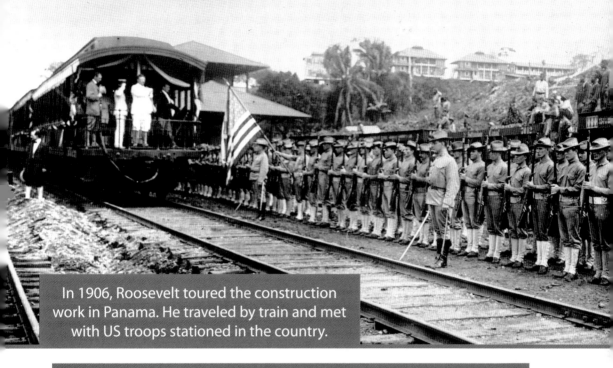

In 1906, Roosevelt toured the construction work in Panama. He traveled by train and met with US troops stationed in the country.

QUICK FACTS

Birth and death: October 27, 1858–January 6, 1919
Wives: Alice (Hathaway Lee) Roosevelt (m. 1880–1884), Edith (Kermit Carow) Roosevelt (m. 1886–1919)
Number of children: Six
Age at inauguration: 42
Years served as president: 1901–1909
Supreme Court appointments: Oliver Wendell Holmes, William Rufus Day, William Henry Moody

Key Cabinet members:
- Vice President: Charles W. Fairbanks
- Secretary of State: John M. Hay, Elihu Root, Robert Bacon
- Secretary of the Treasury: Lyman J. Gage, Leslie M. Shaw, George Cortelyou
- Secretary of War: Elihu Root, William Howard Taft, Luke Wright
- Attorney General: Philander C. Knox, William H. Moody, Charles J. Bonaparte

ROAD TO THE PRESIDENCY

William Howard Taft started his career in law. He served as a judge on several US courts until 1900. That year, President William McKinley asked Taft to help create governments on islands the United States received after the Spanish-American War. Taft excelled in the role and was eventually appointed as a governor in the Philippines. In 1904, President Theodore Roosevelt asked Taft to join his cabinet as the secretary of war, which Taft accepted. Roosevelt admired Taft so much that in 1908, Roosevelt supported Taft's bid for the presidency. Taft, who ran as a Republican, soundly defeated the Democratic candidate William Jennings Bryan.

William Howard Taft always liked law more than politics.

DOLLAR DIPLOMACY

In foreign affairs, Taft pushed policies called "Dollar Diplomacy." These policies encouraged US businesses to invest in Latin America and Asia. Taft believed that US investments would help the governments there become more stable. When governments are unstable, revolutionaries can take over. Stable, peaceful governments benefit everyone.

In 1912, Taft signed legislation that made New Mexico a state.

Taft drew sharp criticism when he dismissed Roosevelt's friend Gifford Pinchot, who was the head of the US Forest Service. Taft fired Pinchot for insubordination after Pinchot criticized both Taft and the head of the US Department of the Interior. Taft's actions hurt his close relationship with Roosevelt. It also tore apart the Republican Party. People had strong opinions when it came to Pinchot's dismissal.

HEADED TO THE SUPREME COURT

Years after he was president, in 1921, Taft was appointed as chief justice of the US Supreme Court by President Warren G. Harding. Serving as the chief justice had been Taft's life goal. He is the only person to have been a US president and a justice on the Supreme Court.

Taft, *center*, was the chief justice of the US Supreme Court until he died in 1930.

Taft, *right*, and Roosevelt had a close relationship until Taft became president. After their falling out, Roosevelt ran against Taft in 1912 for the Republican presidential nomination.

QUICK FACTS

Birth and death: September 15, 1857–March 8, 1930

Wife: Helen (Herron) Taft

Number of children: Three

Age at inauguration: 51

Years served as president: 1909–1913

Supreme Court appointments: Horace Harmon Lurton, Charles Evans Hughes, Edward Douglass White, Willis Van Devanter, Joseph Rucker Lamar, Mahlon Pitney

Key Cabinet members:
- Vice President: James S. Sherman
- Secretary of State: Philander C. Knox
- Secretary of the Treasury: Franklin MacVeagh
- Secretary of War: Jacob M. Dickinson, Henry L. Stimson
- Attorney General: George W. Wickersham

TARIFFS AND BANKS

Woodrow Wilson became president in 1913. He pushed to reduce tariffs and reform banks. Wilson argued that high tariffs hurt consumers and led to monopolies. Wilson also backed the Federal Reserve Act of 1913. The act set up the Federal Reserve System still used today to regulate banks and the money supply. This federal system created regional banks. It had the power to adjust interest rates and the supply of money, as needed. The act was designed to give the country a safer and more stable monetary system.

As president, Woodrow Wilson increased the federal government's role in managing the US economy.

World War I was a brutal war. Experts estimate that more than eight million soldiers and 13 million civilians died during the conflict.

WORLD WAR I

It took years for the United States to get involved in World War I (1914–1918), a conflict that was devastating Europe. During most of the war, the US public did not want to get involved. Wilson honored that. He decided the United States would stay neutral in the conflict.

However, that changed when Germany began attacking US ships traveling to the United Kingdom. In 1917, Wilson asked Congress to declare war on Germany. US soldiers were sent to Europe to join the fight.

LEAGUE OF NATIONS

When World War I ended in 1918, world leaders wanted to develop a peaceful path forward. Wilson traveled to Versailles, France. He worked with foreign leaders to draft the Treaty of Versailles. The treaty harshly punished Germany for its role in the war, but it officially ended the conflict.

Wilson, *right*, met with world leaders during the Treaty of Versailles negotiations.

One of Wilson's suggestions was included in the treaty. He proposed creating a League of Nations. This international group worked together to keep peace and settle disputes around the world. However, Wilson could not convince Congress to join it.

EDITH WILSON

Woodrow Wilson's first wife, Ellen, died early in his first term as president. He later married Edith Bolling Galt. When Woodrow suffered a severe stroke in 1919, Edith stepped up to help him. The First Lady chose what visitors he would see and what papers he would read. Because of her role, some historians describe her as America's first female president.

The League of Nations lasted from 1920 to 1946. More than 40 countries were members.

QUICK FACTS

Birth and death: December 28, 1856–February 3, 1924

Wives: Ellen (Axson) Wilson (m. 1885–1914), Edith (Bolling Galt) Wilson (m. 1915–1924)

Number of children: Three

Age at inauguration: 56

Years served as president: 1913–1921

Supreme Court appointments: James Clark McReynolds, Louis Dembitz Brandeis, John Hessin Clarke

Key Cabinet members:
- Vice President: Thomas R. Marshall
- Secretary of State: William Jennings Bryan, Robert Lansing, Bainbridge Colby
- Secretary of the Treasury: William G. McAdoo, Carter Glass, David Franklin Houston
- Secretary of War: Lindley M. Garrison, Newton Diehl Baker
- Attorney General: James C. McReynolds, Thomas W. Gregory, Alexander Mitchell Palmer

TEAPOT DOME SCANDAL

Warren G. Harding became president in 1921. Although he chose some honorable men for his cabinet, he also gave jobs to dishonest friends. Soon Harding's administration was plagued with scandals. Some people Harding had trusted were charged with defrauding the government. One of these scandals was the Teapot Dome Scandal. Harding's secretary of the interior secretly sold the federal government's oil reserves in Teapot Dome, Wyoming, to oil companies. He collected thousands of dollars in bribes before he was sent to prison. In another scandal, Harding's director of the Veterans Bureau sold drugs intended for veterans' hospitals to narcotics dealers.

Warren G. Harding was a conservative politician who mostly viewed his presidential role as ceremonial.

Charles Forbes was Harding's director of the Veterans Bureau. After discovering what Forbes had done, Harding chastised him and then let him leave the United States to avoid being prosecuted.

HELP FOR FAMILIES

Harding worked to better the lives of women and minorities. He favored equal education and economic opportunities for African Americans. He also spoke out publicly against lynching. His stand against racism was unusual for a politician at this time.

Harding also backed the Sheppard-Towner Maternity and Infancy Protection Act. The act's goal was to lower the death rate among infants and pregnant mothers. This act, passed in 1921, gave funds to states so they could provide health care and health education to pregnant mothers and newborn babies. The death rate among infants dropped as a result of the act.

In the summer of 1923, Harding was in his third year in office. He and his wife took a trip to the western states and Alaska. Harding became ill during the trip with what appeared to be food poisoning. He then died of a heart attack.

Harding promised to bring the United States back to business as usual after World War I.

FLORENCE HARDING

First Lady Florence Harding was a feminist. In 1921, she hosted the world-famous chemist Marie Curie for a White House visit. She also supported the first all-women's tennis tournament at the White House. Florence was able to vote for her husband in the presidential election—the first woman able to do so. This was made possible because in 1920 Congress passed the Nineteenth Amendment, finally giving women the right to vote.

First Lady Florence Harding was very self-reliant and helped advance her husband's political career.

QUICK FACTS

Birth and death: November 2, 1865–August 2, 1923

Wife: Florence (Kling) Harding

Number of children: One child, one stepchild

Age at inauguration: 55

Years served as president: 1921–1923

Supreme Court appointments: William Howard Taft, George Sutherland, Pierce Butler, Edward Terry Sanford

Key Cabinet members:
- Vice President: Calvin Coolidge
- Secretary of State: Charles Evans Hughes
- Secretary of the Treasury: Andrew W. Mellon
- Secretary of War: John W. Weeks
- Attorney General: Harry M. Daugherty

PEACE AND PROSPERITY

After President Warren Harding died in 1923, Vice President Calvin Coolidge became the leader of the United States. The next year, President Coolidge ran for reelection. He won easily.

The 1920s was a period of peace and prosperity in the United States. Coolidge's presidency fell between the brief period after World War I and the Great Depression in the 1930s. The United States experienced economic growth under Coolidge. He also emphasized traditional values along with frugal and thrifty living.

Calvin Coolidge strove to bring back trustworthiness to the executive branch after the previous administration's scandals.

Coolidge was nicknamed "silent Cal" because he was often somber and quiet.

EFFICIENT GOVERNMENT

Coolidge championed an efficient government. His priority was to cut waste, lower federal taxes, and reduce the national debt. However, his economic policies led to imbalances in the US economy. There was an uneven distribution of income. This led to the overproduction of goods, and there weren't enough wealthy people to buy the goods. Eventually, this imbalance contributed to the Great Depression.

IMMIGRATION ACT OF 1924

One major piece of legislation that Coolidge signed was the Immigration Act of 1924. The law placed a limit on immigration. In particular, it limited the number of immigrants coming to the United States from eastern and southern Europe. Immigrants from some parts of Asia were totally banned.

Immigrants come to the United States in search of a better life, but the Immigration Act of 1924 prevented many people from doing that.

Grace Coolidge made up for her husband's quiet demeanor with her friendliness.

QUICK FACTS

Birth and death: July 4, 1872–January 5, 1933
Wife: Grace (Goodhue) Coolidge
Number of children: Two
Age at inauguration: 51
Years served as president: 1923–1929
Supreme Court appointments: Harlan Fiske Stone

Key Cabinet members:
- Vice President: Charles G. Dawes
- Secretary of State: Charles E. Hughes, Frank B. Kellogg
- Secretary of the Treasury: Andrew W. Mellon
- Secretary of War: John W. Weeks, Dwight F. Davis
- Attorney General: Harry M. Daugherty, Harlan Fiske Stone, John G. Sargent

THE GREAT DEPRESSION

Herbert Hoover campaigned for the presidency saying that poverty in the United States was vanishing. Yet eight months after Hoover took office, the stock market crashed. The Great Depression began. It led to a spike in poverty and was the biggest economic crisis the United States had experienced.

The Great Depression lasted from 1929 to 1939. Many people lost their jobs. Some couldn't pay for their homes and were forced to live on the streets. Shacks and tent camps popped up in cities.

Before he was president, Herbert Hoover was known for his work as an engineer and humanitarian.

The camps where homeless people lived were called Hoovervilles. People there blamed Hoover for the depression.

During the economic crisis, Hoover supported plans that helped businesses and farmers. He gave money to states to feed people who had lost their jobs. Yet he also believed local governments and volunteers were responsible for helping people who were suffering. He did not think the federal government should get too deeply involved. People criticized Hoover for not doing enough to help Americans.

GOOD NEIGHBOR POLICY

When it came to foreign affairs, Hoover worked to establish good relations with other countries through negotiations. He did not want to use military force. One example of this is Hoover's Good Neighbor Policy toward South and Central American countries. Hoover promised that the United States would stay out of Latin American affairs by reducing US political and military involvement and would be a "good neighbor." This Good Neighbor Policy continued into the next administration.

Hoover's presidency was ultimately defined by the Great Depression.

Lou and Herbert Hoover traveled around the globe together, visiting Australia, Japan, Egypt, and the European continent.

QUICK FACTS

Birth and death: August 10, 1874–October 20, 1964

Wife: Lou (Henry) Hoover

Number of children: Two

Age at inauguration: 54

Years served as president: 1929–1933

Supreme Court appointments: Charles Evans Hughes, Owen Josephus Roberts, Benjamin Nathan Cardozo

Key Cabinet members:
- Vice President: Charles Curtis
- Secretary of State: Henry L. Stimson
- Secretary of the Treasury: Andrew W. Mellon, Ogden L. Mills
- Secretary of War: James W. Good, Patrick J. Hurley
- Attorney General: William DeWitt Mitchell

THE NEW DEAL

Franklin D. Roosevelt was elected president four times. His presidency spanned 12 years. No other US president has served that long. Roosevelt came into office in 1933. He enacted a New Deal program to help get the United States out of the Great Depression. The New Deal created new government agencies. These helped Americans in areas such as housing, finance, and agriculture. The New Deal gave unemployed people jobs. They built structures such as schools, libraries, and bridges. Farmers received financial help. Workers got higher wages. Banks became more stable.

In 1921, Franklin D. Roosevelt contracted polio. This disease left his legs paralyzed. He tried to hide his use of a wheelchair from the public and wore leg braces to help him stand upright.

The New Deal also set up social welfare programs. These helped older citizens, the poor, and the unemployed. The programs did not fully solve the problems of the Great Depression. But they did provide much-needed help

In 1933, Roosevelt signed the Emergency Banking Act. This act aimed to build people's confidence in the US banking system during the Great Depression.

to the American people. The United States finally pulled out of the depression around 1939 as World War II (1939–1945) began.

WORLD WAR II

When Roosevelt was elected to his third term in 1940, World War II had already started. For a while, the United States remained neutral in the conflict, which spanned across Europe and the Pacific. That changed after Japan attacked Pearl Harbor in 1941. Pearl Harbor is a US naval base in Hawaii. During the attack, Japan destroyed many US military aircraft and ships. This action drew the United States into the war. It chose to fight against Japan in the Pacific and against Nazi Germany in Europe. During this time, Roosevelt rallied US support for the fight.

In the later years of the war, Roosevelt worked toward peace. He supported the United Nations organization that formed in 1945. The United Nations is an international group with many member countries. These countries meet and work together to promote peace and friendly relations. Roosevelt believed the United Nations was the best way to prevent conflicts in the future. In 1945, Roosevelt died while still in office. His vice president, Harry S. Truman, took over.

Fighting a war on two fronts was a massive undertaking that required careful planning and communication.

ELEANOR ROOSEVELT

Eleanor Roosevelt brought energy and activism to the job of First Lady. She championed civil rights issues, worked to help the unemployed, and pushed for women's involvement in politics. She traveled to the poorest parts of the country to learn how the Great Depression was impacting the people there. After leaving the White House, she continued her work for human rights as a US delegate to the United Nations General Assembly. She also served as chair of the commission on human rights for the Economic and Social Council.

In 1945, Roosevelt met with British prime minister Winston Churchill, *left*, and Soviet Union premier Joseph Stalin, *right*, to discuss World War II.

QUICK FACTS

Birth and death: January 30, 1882–April 12, 1945
Wife: Anna Eleanor Roosevelt
Number of children: Six
Age at inauguration: 51
Years served as president: 1933–1945
Supreme Court appointments: Hugo Lafayette Black, Stanley Forman Reed, Felix Frankfurter, William Orville Douglas, Frank Murphy, Harlan Fiske Stone, James Francis Byrnes, Robert Houghwout Jackson, Wiley Blount Rutledge

Key Cabinet members:
- Vice President: John N. Garner, Henry A. Wallace, Harry S. Truman
- Secretary of State: Cordell Hull, Edward R. Stettinius Jr.
- Secretary of the Treasury: William H. Woodin, Henry Morgenthau Jr.
- Secretary of War: George H. Dern, Harry H. Woodring, Henry L. Stimson
- Attorney General: Homer S. Cummings, Frank Murphy, Robert H. Jackson, Francis B. Biddle

ATOMIC BOMBS

Harry S. Truman became president near the end of World War II. To end this conflict, in August 1945, Truman authorized the use of the newly developed atomic bombs on two cities in Japan. These bombs were the most powerful weapons the world had ever seen. Truman hoped dropping the bombs would force Japan to surrender. Historians estimate that more than 170,000 Japanese people died. Truman's decision to use the bombs ended the war. But it came with a tremendous loss of human life.

Harry S. Truman was vice president for just 82 days before President Franklin D. Roosevelt died in 1945.

The United States dropped atomic bombs on Hiroshima and Nagasaki. Many people were maimed or killed, and the cities were unrecognizable.

THE COLD WAR BEGINS

After World War II ended, the United States and the Soviet Union emerged as the world's two superpowers. Tensions were high between them. The two countries had very different systems of government and ways of doing things. As a result, the United States and the Soviet Union entered what is called the Cold War. Their militaries never directly fought. Instead, the countries tried to outperform each other in different ways.

Truman promised that the United States would stop the Soviet Union's way of government—Communism—from spreading. This did not help tensions between the two countries. Truman's promise laid the foundation for US foreign policy for decades to come. Many future presidents also tried to stop the spread of Communism.

SUPPORT FOR NEW DEAL REFORMS

At home, Truman supported Roosevelt's New Deal reforms. Truman raised the minimum wage. He expanded programs to help people who were not working. In addition, Truman supported civil rights for African Americans and desegregated the US military. Truman led the country out of World War II and into peacetime. He helped build a healthy economy that would grow over the next two decades.

In 1947, Truman asked Congress for money to help certain eastern European countries. He worried that without this help the countries would turn to Communism.

In 1949, Truman declared February 1 as National Freedom Day. This day celebrates the Thirteenth Amendment, which outlawed slavery.

QUICK FACTS

Birth and death: May 8, 1884–December 26, 1972
Wife: Elizabeth (Wallace) Truman
Number of children: One
Age at inauguration: 60
Years served as president: 1945–1953
Supreme Court appointments: Harold Hitz Burton, Fred Moore Vinson, Tom Campbell Clark, Sherman Minton
Key Cabinet members:
- Vice President: Alben W. Barkley

- Secretary of State: Edward R. Stettinius Jr., James Byrnes, George C. Marshall, Dean Acheson
- Secretary of the Treasury: Henry Morgenthau Jr., Frederick M. Vinson, John W. Snyder
- Secretary of War/Defense: Robert P. Patterson, Kenneth C. Royall, Henry L. Stimson
- Attorney General: Francis Biddle, Thomas C. Clark, J. Howard McGrath, James P. McGranery

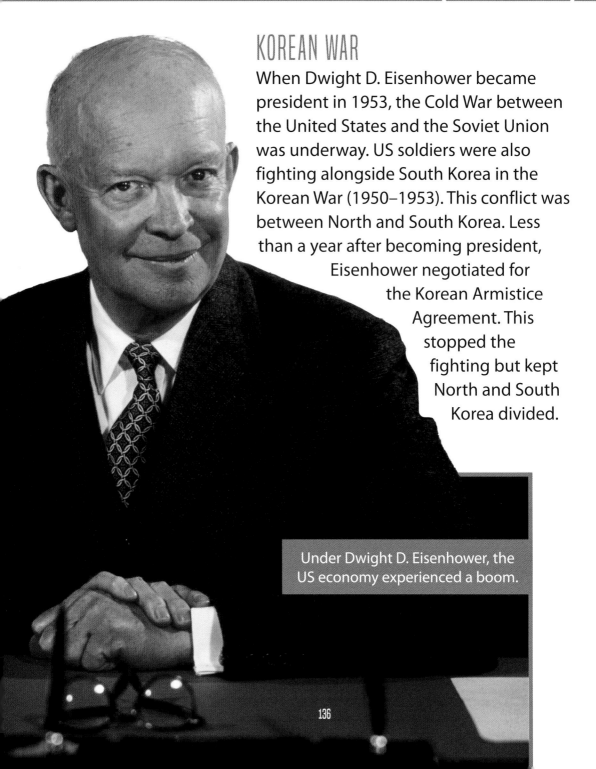

34TH
DWIGHT D. EISENHOWER (1953–1961)

KOREAN WAR

When Dwight D. Eisenhower became president in 1953, the Cold War between the United States and the Soviet Union was underway. US soldiers were also fighting alongside South Korea in the Korean War (1950–1953). This conflict was between North and South Korea. Less than a year after becoming president, Eisenhower negotiated for the Korean Armistice Agreement. This stopped the fighting but kept North and South Korea divided.

Under Dwight D. Eisenhower, the US economy experienced a boom.

136

Some highway construction, such as the Cross-Bronx Expressway in New York, purposefully cut through minority communities, breaking them apart.

ROADS ACROSS AMERICA

In 1956, Eisenhower set up the Interstate Highway system. Before this system was created, many US roads were in poor condition. Even the paved roads were bumpy and rough. This led to flat tires and broken parts on cars. In addition, many bridges were only large enough to allow cars to cross, so trucks could not use them. Eisenhower's Interstate Highway program built 41,000 miles (65,980 km) of roads across the United States. The new system of roads made it easier for people to travel and for goods to be moved across the country. Building the roads provided jobs for many people. The new highway system led to a booming US economy.

LITTLE ROCK NINE AND VOTING RIGHTS

In 1957, a white school named Central High School in Little Rock, Arkansas, was desegregated. That meant people of color could attend the school. Many white people were unhappy with this, including Arkansas governor Orval Faubus. On September 2, 1957, the day before nine African American students were set to attend the school, Faubus sent in the National Guard. They blocked the Black students' access to the school.

Eisenhower tried to reason with Faubus, but the governor was unmoved. As a result, Eisenhower took control of the Arkansas National Guard. Then he sent in 1,000 US Army troops to make sure the nine Black students got into the school.

Elizabeth Eckford of the Little Rock Nine was harassed by her fellow students when she tried to go to school.

That month, Eisenhower signed the Civil Rights Act of 1957. This law protected people's voting rights. It also showed how committed the US government was to protecting people of all races.

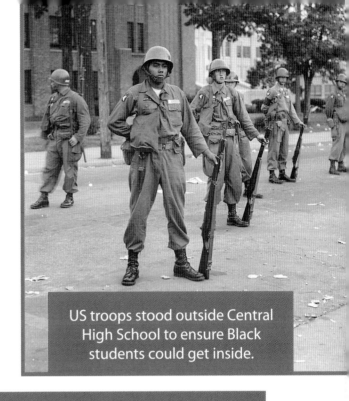

US troops stood outside Central High School to ensure Black students could get inside.

QUICK FACTS

Birth and death: October 14, 1890–March 28, 1969
Wife: Mamie (Doud) Eisenhower
Number of children: Two
Age at inauguration: 62
Years served as president: 1953–1961
Supreme Court appointments: Earl Warren, John Marshall Harlan, William J. Brennan Jr., Charles Evans Whittaker, Potter Stewart

Key Cabinet members:
- Vice President: Richard Nixon
- Secretary of State: John Foster Dulles, Christian A. Herter
- Secretary of the Treasury: George M. Humphrey, Robert B. Anderson
- Secretary of Defense: Charles E. Wilson, Neil H. McElroy, Thomas S. Gates Jr.
- Attorney General: Herbert Brownell Jr., William P. Rogers

A YOUNG PRESIDENT

At age 43, John F. Kennedy was the youngest person ever elected president. He took office in 1961 but didn't finish his first term. An assassin killed him on November 22, 1963.

THE BAY OF PIGS

In 1961, the United States wanted to overthrow the Cuban government. Cuba's leader, Fidel Castro, was on good terms with the Soviet Union. At the time, the United States and the Soviet Union were in the middle of the Cold War. The United States did not want a friend of the Soviet Union so close to US borders.

John F. Kennedy first served in the US House of Representatives in 1947 for the state of Massachusetts. Then he joined the US Senate in 1953.

140

Cuban forces confiscated the exiles'
weapons during the failed invasion.

US forces trained Cuban exiles. They wanted the exiles to
invade Cuba and take down Castro's government. In April
1961, the Bay of Pigs invasion began. It did not go as planned.
Castro's troops captured many of the exiles. His government
was not overturned. The failure was an embarrassment to the
Kennedy administration.

THE CUBAN MISSILE CRISIS

After the Bay of Pigs, the Soviet Union decided to send nuclear missiles to Cuba. Both countries hoped it would stop the United States from attempting another invasion. But the United States found out the Cubans were building missile sites and that the country was getting weapons from the Soviet Union. This news alarmed Kennedy. He did not want an unfriendly neighbor to have weapons that could be launched at the United States.

In October 1962, Kennedy placed a naval quarantine around Cuba. He did this to stop the Soviet Union from sending any more supplies to Cuba. Kennedy also contacted the leader of the Soviet Union, Nikita Khrushchev. Kennedy told him that the weapons in Cuba needed to leave. Khrushchev, for his part, viewed Kennedy's naval quarantine as an aggressive move. Tensions were high. The two countries were on the edge of a nuclear war. However, the two leaders talked and worked out a deal, avoiding war.

Kennedy intentionally used the term *quarantine* for the naval action around Cuba. Calling it a blockade would have suggested that Cuba and the United States were at war.

Kennedy was riding in an open car in Dallas, Texas, when an assassin shot him.

QUICK FACTS

Birth and death: May 29, 1917–November 22, 1963

Wife: Jacqueline (Bouvier) Kennedy Onassis

Number of children: Three

Age at inauguration: 43

Years served as president: 1961–1963

Supreme Court appointments: Byron Raymond White, Arthur Joseph Goldberg

Key Cabinet members:
- Vice President: Lyndon B. Johnson
- Secretary of State: Dean Rusk
- Secretary of the Treasury: C. Douglas Dillon
- Secretary of Defense: Robert S. McNamara
- Attorney General: Robert F. Kennedy

GREAT SOCIETY

Lyndon B. Johnson was vice president when President John F. Kennedy was killed in November 1963. Johnson wanted to create a prosperous society for all Americans. As president, his Great Society program provided aid for education and health care. It focused on renewing the cities by building affordable housing. It also pushed conservation efforts to protect water, air, and wilderness areas. In addition, the program fought poverty and crime.

Lyndon B. Johnson helped push through legislation that his predecessor, President John F. Kennedy, had wanted passed. This included a tax cut and a civil rights bill.

144

Johnson signed the Civil Rights Act of 1964 before a crowd of onlookers.

JOHNSON AND CIVIL RIGHTS

Johnson signed the Civil Rights Act of 1964. This law made discrimination in public spaces illegal. It also banned discrimination in employment due to a person's religion, sex, race, color, or national origin.

Next, Johnson backed the Voting Rights Act of 1965. This law ended literacy tests used to stop some African Americans from voting. Both the Civil Rights Act and the Voting Rights Act aimed to make sure all Americans were treated equally. However, discrimination against people of color still continued, and between 1964 and 1968, race riots occurred in many US cities. Johnson responded to the unrest by setting up a commission to study the problem. After months of work, the commission reported that poverty and racism were causes of the violence. But Johnson did not act to address these things.

VIETNAM WAR

In addition to the racial unrest in the country, Johnson also faced anti-war protests related to the Vietnam War (1954–1975). North Vietnam had a Communist government. It was trying to take control of South Vietnam, which had a non-Communist government. US troops supported South Vietnam. During the war, millions of Vietnamese people died. More than 58,000 US military personnel were killed. It was the most unpopular war in US history. Johnson had promised Americans that he would not expand US involvement in the war. Yet he increased the number of US troops in Vietnam.

Detroit, Michigan, was the site of one race riot in 1967. The riot lasted for five days, and around 1,000 buildings were burned. Forty-three people died.

US soldiers had to navigate difficult terrain while in Vietnam.

QUICK FACTS

Birth and death: August 27, 1908–January 22, 1973

Wife: Claudia Alta (Taylor) Johnson

Number of children: Two

Age at inauguration: 55

Years served as president: 1963–1969

Supreme Court appointments: Abe Fortas, Thurgood Marshall

Key Cabinet members:
- Vice President: Hubert Humphrey
- Secretary of State: Dean Rusk
- Secretary of the Treasury: C. Douglas Dillon, Henry H. Fowler, Joseph Barr
- Secretary of Defense: Robert S. McNamara, Clark Clifford
- Attorney General: Robert F. Kennedy, Nicholas Katzenbach, Ramsey Clark

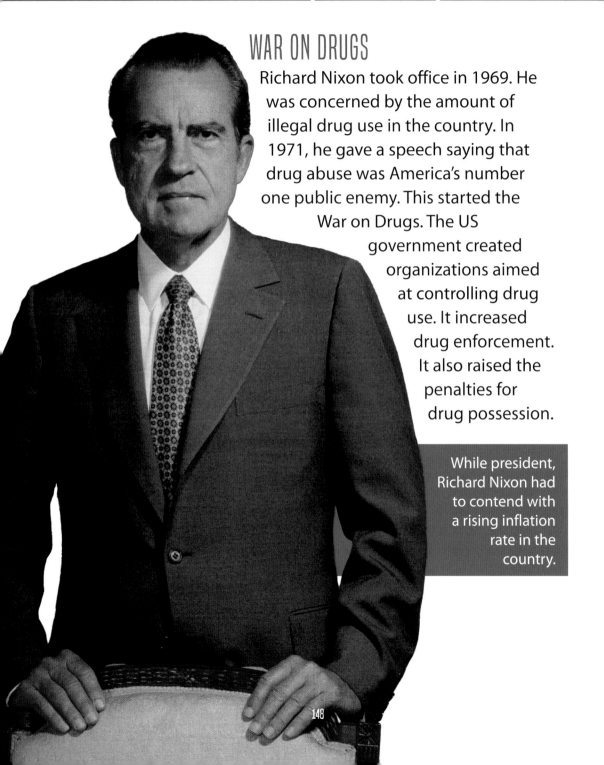

WAR ON DRUGS

Richard Nixon took office in 1969. He was concerned by the amount of illegal drug use in the country. In 1971, he gave a speech saying that drug abuse was America's number one public enemy. This started the War on Drugs. The US government created organizations aimed at controlling drug use. It increased drug enforcement. It also raised the penalties for drug possession.

While president, Richard Nixon had to contend with a rising inflation rate in the country.

Before Nixon's visit to China, no US president had visited the country since the 1940s.

The War on Drugs has lasted for decades. Hundreds of thousands of people have been arrested. The US government has spent more than $1 trillion on fighting the drug war. But it has not stopped drug use in the United States. In addition, the War on Drugs unfairly targets people of color. It's for these reasons experts say the War on Drugs has failed.

SIGNIFICANT AGENCIES

In 1970, Nixon signed laws establishing the Environmental Protection Agency (EPA) and the National Oceanic and Atmospheric Administration (NOAA). The EPA was created to enforce national guidelines that protect the environment from pollution. NOAA studies climate and the oceans to protect coastal areas and marine environments. In addition, Nixon signed legislation that created the Occupational Safety and Health Administration (OSHA). This organization makes sure people have safe working environments.

BUILDING PEACE

One of Nixon's great achievements was his work on building better relations with China and the Soviet Union. In 1972, Nixon traveled to Communist China and met with leaders there. With this historic trip, Nixon began rebuilding US relations with China.

In strengthening Soviet relations, Nixon and Soviet leader Leonid Brezhnev signed the Anti-Ballistic Missile Treaty in 1972. This treaty limited missile defense systems in both countries. In addition, in 1973, Nixon worked out a peace agreement that ended the conflict between the United States and North Vietnam.

WATERGATE SCANDAL

The Watergate scandal happened during the 1972 presidential campaign. There was a break-in at the Democratic National Committee offices. The men who broke in were trying to bug the office and spy on the people inside.

Evidence showed the men were linked to Nixon's campaign. Nixon tried to hide his part in the crime. As the facts came to light, Nixon faced impeachment. However, before Congress could impeach him, Nixon resigned on August 8, 1974. He is the only president to resign while in office.

The Senate created a committee to investigate the Watergate scandal.

QUICK FACTS

Birth and death: January 9, 1913–April 22, 1994
Wife: Thelma (Ryan) Nixon
Number of children: Two
Age at inauguration: 56
Years served as president: 1969–1974
Supreme Court appointments: Warren Earl Burger, Harry A. Blackmun, Lewis F. Powell Jr., William H. Rehnquist
Key Cabinet members:
  • Vice President: Spiro T. Agnew, Gerald Ford

• Secretary of State: William P. Rogers, Henry Kissinger
• Secretary of the Treasury: David M. Kennedy, John B. Connally, George P. Shultz, William E. Simon
• Secretary of Defense: Melvin R. Laird, Elliot L. Richardson, James R. Schlesinger
• Attorney General: John N. Mitchell, Richard G. Kleindienst, Elliot L. Richardson, William B. Saxbe

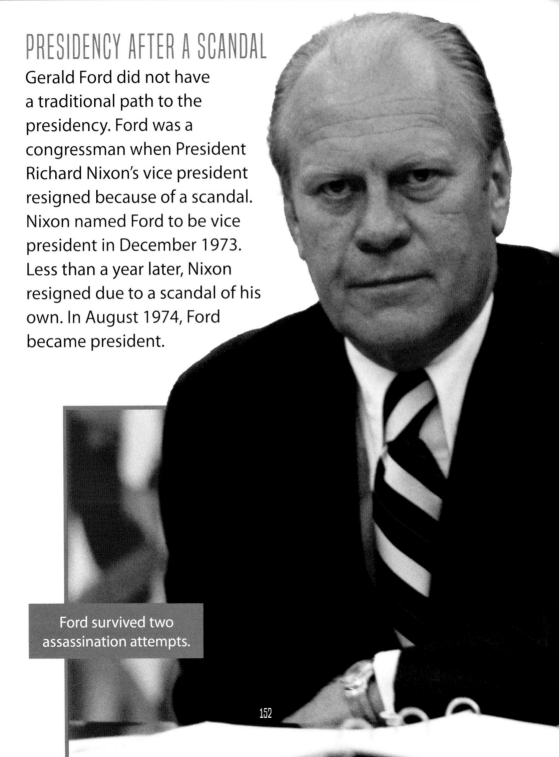

38TH
GERALD FORD (1974–1977)

PRESIDENCY AFTER A SCANDAL

Gerald Ford did not have a traditional path to the presidency. Ford was a congressman when President Richard Nixon's vice president resigned because of a scandal. Nixon named Ford to be vice president in December 1973. Less than a year later, Nixon resigned due to a scandal of his own. In August 1974, Ford became president.

Ford survived two assassination attempts.

People waited in long lines outside gas stations in the hopes of being able to get gas.

THE US ECONOMY

When Ford took office, the country faced severe economic challenges. Unemployment and inflation were rising. In 1973, just before Ford became president, several Arab countries placed an oil embargo on the United States. This created a gasoline shortage and high gas prices in the country. To fight inflation, Ford proposed raising taxes and reducing federal spending. Later, Ford proposed cutting taxes to help boost the economy. People criticized Ford for his flip-flop on taxes. They felt he was not managing the economic problems effectively.

FOREIGN AFFAIRS SUCCESSES

When it came to foreign affairs, Ford negotiated with the Soviet Union to control the building of nuclear weapons. In addition, he also provided aid to Israel and Egypt to help prevent a war in the Middle East. Ford's administration also worked to convince Israel and Egypt to accept a truce agreement, maintaining peace between the two countries. In addition, the Vietnam War was ending. Ford evacuated the last Americans remaining in Vietnam in 1975.

Ford met with Israeli prime minister Yitzhak Rabin, *right*, in 1974 and assured him of the United States' support for Israel.

First Lady Betty Ford had breast cancer surgery in 1974. She spoke about her experience to the public and encouraged other women to speak up about their health struggles too.

BETTY FORD

Elizabeth "Betty" Ford used her position as First Lady to speak about topics that were important to her. She advocated for women and the Equal Rights Amendment that aimed to guarantee women the same legal rights as men. Betty also opened up about her battle with breast cancer. After leaving the White House, she received treatment for prescription drug and alcohol use. Following treatment, Betty became a champion for people in recovery from alcohol and drug addiction. Through her open conversations, she educated people about these important topics.

QUICK FACTS

Birth and death: July 14, 1913–December 26, 2006
Wife: Elizabeth (Bloomer) Ford
Number of children: Four
Age at inauguration: 61
Years served as president: 1974–1977
Supreme Court appointments: John Paul Stevens
Key Cabinet members:
- Vice President: Nelson A. Rockefeller

- Secretary of State: Henry A. Kissinger
- Secretary of the Treasury: William E. Simon
- Secretary of Defense: James R. Schlesinger, Donald H. Rumsfeld
- Attorney General: Edward H. Levi, William B. Saxbe

CHALLENGES AND ACHIEVEMENTS

James "Jimmy" Carter entered office in 1977. He worked to solve unemployment and inflation. Carter reduced the budget deficit. He added almost eight million jobs for Americans. But inflation and interest rates remained high. They were difficult challenges for Carter.

Jimmy Carter started his career in the US Navy before getting into politics.

Carter signed a bill creating the US Department of Energy in 1977.

Carter also had to manage an ongoing energy crisis that had begun in the early 1970s. Carter developed a national energy policy. He created the US Department of Energy. This agency explored types of energy other than oil. In 1978, Carter signed his first energy package into law. His goal was to lower the country's dependence on oil. Carter also wanted to increase the use of renewable energy sources such as solar power. He even had solar panels installed on the White House roof to heat the water in the building.

VICTORIES AND STRUGGLES ABROAD

In foreign policy, Carter's greatest achievement was the Camp David Accords. These were peace talks between leaders from Israel and Egypt. They took place in the late 1970s. These two countries had been in conflict with each other. Carter invited them to the United States for negotiations. The Camp David Accords led to the Egyptian-Israeli Peace Treaty. In 2002, Carter received the Nobel Peace Prize for his work in solving international conflicts and advancing human rights.

Carter, Egyptian president Anwar Sadat, *left*, and Israeli prime minister Menachem Begin, *right*, celebrated a peace treaty between Egypt and Israel in 1979.

More than 50 Americans were held hostage during the Iranian Hostage Crisis.

Carter faced struggles abroad too. In late 1979, Iranian students seized the US Embassy staff in Iran and held them hostage for 444 days. Carter sent a military team to rescue the hostages. That mission failed, and some of the military personnel were killed. This event had a negative impact in the last year of Carter's presidency. Carter ran for president in 1980 but was not reelected.

QUICK FACTS

Birth: October 1, 1924
Wife: Rosalynn (Smith) Carter
Number of children: Four
Age at inauguration: 52
Years served as president: 1977–1981
Key Cabinet members:
- Vice President: Walter Mondale

- Secretary of State: Cyrus Vance, Edmund Muskie
- Secretary of the Treasury: W. Michael Blumenthal, G. William Miller
- Secretary of Defense: Harold Brown
- Attorney General: Griffin Bell, Benjamin Civiletti

A HOPEFUL CAMPAIGN

When Ronald Reagan took office in 1981, the American people's confidence in government was low. People were weary of economic problems like inflation, unemployment, and the energy crisis. Reagan campaigned with hopeful ideas for the future.

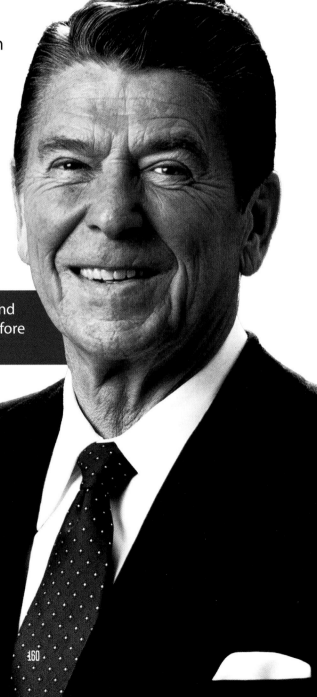

Ronald Reagan was an actor and then governor of California before becoming president.

Reagan discussed the Iran-Contra Affair with congressional leaders, who organized committees to investigate the situation.

IRAN-CONTRA AFFAIR

In the 1980s, Reagan faced heavy criticism for the Iran-Contra Affair. This was a political scandal. In 1985, the Reagan administration secretly authorized weapons sales to Iran in exchange for the release of US hostages held by Iranian terrorists. Some of the money from the sales was then given to rebels fighting in Nicaragua—something the US Congress had prohibited. In 1986, a newspaper exposed what Reagan's administration had done. Despite the scandal, Reagan left office in 1989 with a high approval rating.

SUCCESSES AND STRUGGLES

In the 1980s, people were contracting acquired immunodeficiency syndrome (AIDS) and dying from it. At the start of the crisis, people didn't know much about AIDS. The government response was slow, and Reagan faced criticism.

When Reagan took office, the United States was struggling with high taxes, interest rates, and unemployment. Reagan helped the US economy with the 1981 Economic Recovery Tax Act, which reduced taxes and helped small businesses. In addition, in 1986, Reagan overhauled the income tax system. This Tax Reform Act of 1986 was designed to simplify the income tax code and make taxes fairer for people. It was Reagan's biggest achievement at home during his second term.

At times during the Cold War, Reagan worked with Soviet Union president Mikhail Gorbachev. In 1987, the two leaders signed the Intermediate-Range Nuclear Forces Treaty. Under this treaty, both countries eliminated medium- and intermediate-range missiles that could carry nuclear weapons.

By the end of Reagan's presidency, the country was enjoying peacetime prosperity and economic growth. In addition, Reagan had nominated the first woman to the US Supreme Court: Sandra Day O'Connor.

Sandra Day O'Connor, *right*, joined the US Supreme Court on September 25, 1981—a little more than two months after Reagan had nominated her.

QUICK FACTS

Birth and death: February 6, 1911–June 5, 2004

Wives: Jane Wyman (m. 1940–1948), Nancy (Davis) Reagan (m. 1952–2004)

Number of children: Four

Age at inauguration: 69

Years served as president: 1981–1989

Supreme Court appointments: Sandra Day O'Connor, William H. Rehnquist, Antonin Scalia, Anthony Kennedy

Key Cabinet members:
- Vice President: George H. W. Bush
- Secretary of State: Alexander Haig Jr., George Shultz
- Secretary of the Treasury: Donald Regan, James Baker, Nicholas F. Brady
- Secretary of Defense: Caspar Weinberger, Frank Carlucci
- Attorney General: Edwin Meese, Richard Thornburgh, William French Smith

THE PERSIAN GULF WAR

George H. W. Bush became president in 1989. He faced a big foreign policy challenge when Iraq invaded the small Middle Eastern country of Kuwait in 1990. Kuwait has a lot of oil. At the time, Iraq wanted this oil. It also wanted to expand its power in the Middle East.

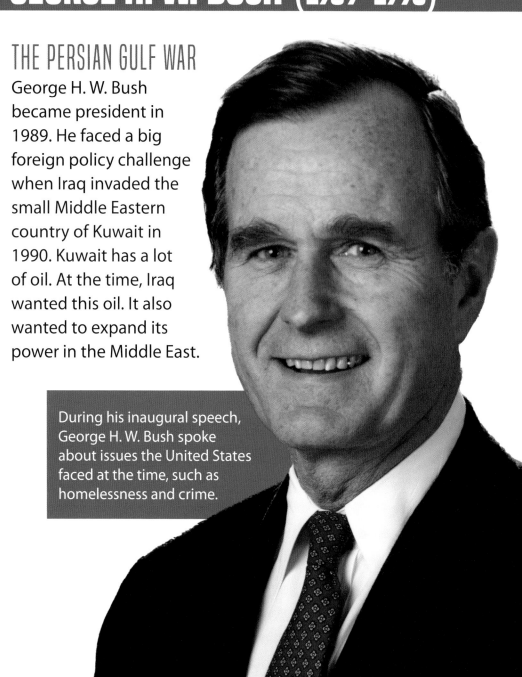

During his inaugural speech, George H. W. Bush spoke about issues the United States faced at the time, such as homelessness and crime.

Bush visited US soldiers during the Persian Gulf War.

The international community was outraged by the invasion. Bush and the United States led the charge to free Kuwait. Both US and international troops began attacking Iraqi forces. This conflict was called the Persian Gulf War (1990–1991), and Iraq was defeated and pushed out of Kuwait. People view the success of this operation as a highlight of Bush's presidency.

HELPING THE AMERICAN PEOPLE

In 1990, Bush backed two important laws. First, he signed the Americans with Disabilities Act. This law protected people with disabilities from discrimination in the workplace. It also said public buildings and areas needed to be made accessible to people with disabilities.

Wheelchair ramps are one example of how public buildings can be made accessible.

That same year, Bush signed amendments to the Clean Air Act. The amendments protected both people's health and the environment. They addressed environmental threats including air pollution and acid rain.

TAXES RAISED

When Bush became president, the federal debt was $2.8 trillion. Bush had promised he would not raise taxes. But he needed to in order to balance the budget and reduce the debt. This reversal made Bush unpopular with many voters. Bush did not win reelection for a second term.

Barbara Bush championed literacy and also focused on fighting homelessness and AIDS.

BARBARA BUSH

As First Lady, Barbara Bush aimed to improve literacy in the United States. She believed that if more people knew how to read, other problems such as drug abuse, crime, and teen pregnancy would also improve. Barbara helped to pass the National Literacy Act. This act focused on teaching millions of adults to read. Barbara wrote two children's books and visited schools to talk about the power of reading.

QUICK FACTS

Birth and death: June 12, 1924–November 30, 2018
Wife: Barbara (Pierce) Bush
Number of children: Six
Age at inauguration: 64
Years served as president: 1989–1993
Supreme Court appointments: David H. Souter, Clarence Thomas

Key Cabinet members:
- Vice President: Dan Quayle
- Secretary of State: James A. Baker, Lawrence Eagleburger
- Secretary of the Treasury: Nicholas F. Brady
- Secretary of Defense: Richard B. Cheney
- Attorney General: Richard L. Thornburgh, William P. Barr

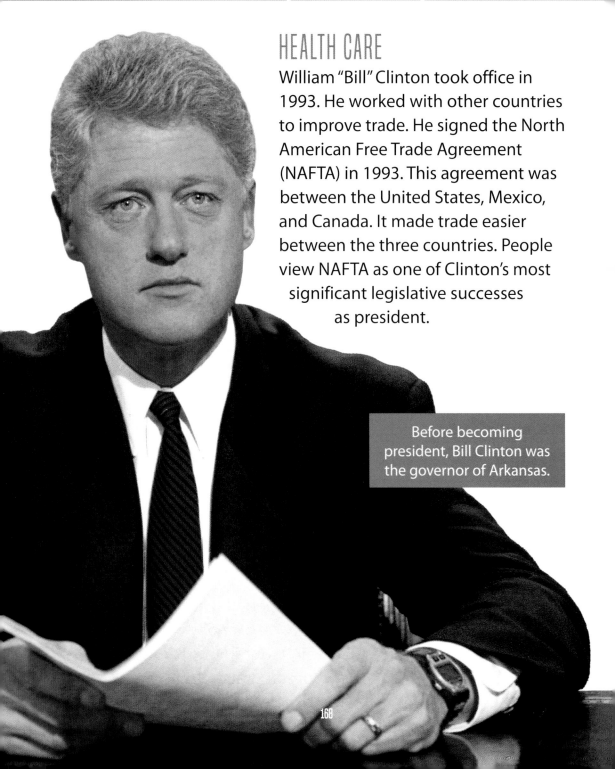

HEALTH CARE

William "Bill" Clinton took office in 1993. He worked with other countries to improve trade. He signed the North American Free Trade Agreement (NAFTA) in 1993. This agreement was between the United States, Mexico, and Canada. It made trade easier between the three countries. People view NAFTA as one of Clinton's most significant legislative successes as president.

Before becoming president, Bill Clinton was the governor of Arkansas.

By signing NAFTA, Clinton created the largest free-trade area in the world.

INTERNATIONAL CONFLICTS

In 1994, mass killings were occurring in Rwanda. The Hutus in the country were committing genocide against the Tutsis, murdering hundreds of thousands of people. Despite this, Clinton was hesitant to get involved. He did not want to send US soldiers to Africa. Not intervening to stop the genocide proved to be one of Clinton's biggest regrets.

Also during Clinton's presidency, the European country of Bosnia and Herzegovina was reeling from violence. In 1995, Serbs in the country were murdering Muslims. Clinton worked with member countries in the North Atlantic Treaty Organization (NATO), of which the United States was a member, to stop the violence. NATO unleashed an international military force on Bosnia and Herzegovina. It conducted air strikes on the country and ultimately stopped the Serbs.

One NATO air strike campaign, Operation Deliberate Force, lasted more than two weeks and greatly hurt Serb communications.

SCANDAL AND IMPEACHMENT

While in office, Clinton had an inappropriate relationship with a young White House intern named Monica Lewinsky. When the scandal was brought to light, Clinton lied under oath. The US House of Representatives impeached him for perjury and for obstruction of justice. The Senate found him not guilty, and he remained in office.

Hillary Clinton has been the First Lady, a US senator, and the US secretary of state. She was also the 2016 Democratic nominee for president.

QUICK FACTS

Birth: August 19, 1946
Wife: Hillary (Rodham) Clinton
Number of children: One
Age at inauguration: 46
Years served as president: 1993–2001
Supreme Court appointments: Ruth Bader Ginsburg, Stephen G. Breyer
Key Cabinet members:
- Vice President: Al Gore Jr.
- Secretary of State: Warren M. Christopher, Madeleine Albright
- Secretary of the Treasury: Lloyd Bentsen, Robert Rubin, Lawrence Summers
- Secretary of Defense: Les Aspin, William J. Perry, William Cohen
- Attorney General: Janet Reno

SEPTEMBER 11 ATTACKS

George W. Bush became president in 2001. At the start of his presidency, Bush and the United States faced a major crisis. On September 11, 2001, terrorists from an organization based in Afghanistan attacked various areas in the United States. They hijacked planes. Some flew the planes into buildings. Almost 3,000 people died in the terrorist attacks.

George W. Bush's father is former president George H. W. Bush.

Bush visited the site of the attack, known as Ground Zero.

The Twin Towers in New York City were two targets hit by the hijackers.

The events on September 11 shaped Bush's presidency. He vowed to fight terrorism to protect the United States. Suddenly, Bush was a wartime president. He sent US troops to Afghanistan and later Iraq. The US public supported Bush for his actions just after the terrorist attacks. Polls taken during that time showed he had a 90 percent approval rating. This rating made him the most popular president since polling began in the early 1930s. After September 11, Bush also restructured US security programs and signed the PATRIOT Act. These changes made it easier for the US government and military to search for and hold suspected terrorists.

EDUCATION REFORM

While president, Bush signed the No Child Left Behind Act. This 2002 act reformed the US education system. It set a national curriculum and testing standards. Its goal was to bring all students to the same levels in math, reading, and writing. The act was passed with bipartisan support. But some people criticized it as being too focused on testing and school report cards. A new plan replaced the act in 2015.

HURRICANE KATRINA

Hurricane Katrina struck Louisiana and the Gulf Coast in August 2005. The damage it left behind was immense. It was the country's most costly natural disaster. The federal government sent relief supplies. But the disaster overwhelmed the people of that region. Critics accused Bush of not doing enough to help people affected by the hurricane.

Weeks after Hurricane Katrina, sections of New Orleans were still covered in floodwater.

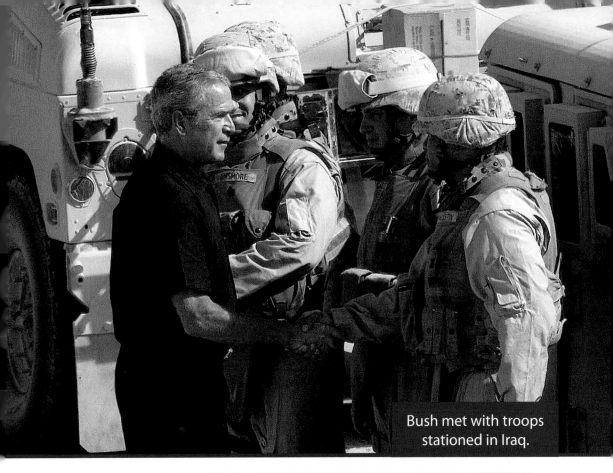

Bush met with troops stationed in Iraq.

QUICK FACTS

Birth: July 6, 1946

Wife: Laura (Welch) Bush

Number of children: Two

Age at inauguration: 54

Years served as president: 2001–2009

Supreme Court appointments: John Roberts, Samuel Alito

Key Cabinet members:
- Vice President: Richard B. Cheney
- Secretary of State: Colin L. Powell, Condoleezza Rice
- Secretary of the Treasury: Paul H. O'Neill, John W. Snow, Henry M. Paulson Jr.
- Secretary of Defense: Donald H. Rumsfeld, Robert M. Gates
- Attorney General: John Ashcroft, Alberto Gonzales, Michael B. Mukasey

THE ECONOMY AND HEALTH CARE

In 2009, Barack Obama became president. He was the first Black person to hold the position. When Obama took office, the country was in a recession. It was the biggest downturn in the US economy since the Great Depression. In 2009, Obama backed the American Recovery and Reinvestment Act. This was an $800 billion economic plan. It was designed to create jobs for people and boost the economy. It helped rebuild the economy, especially the auto industry. However, it pushed the federal deficit up to more than $1 trillion a year.

Before becoming president, Barack Obama was a lawyer, a community organizer, an Illinois state senator, and a US senator.

Obama signed the Affordable Care Act on March 23, 2010.

Obama also signed the Affordable Care Act in 2010. This act reformed the health-care system. It provided affordable health insurance to many people. However, the Affordable Care Act proved controversial, as some people didn't want the federal government to expand its power into the health-care system.

THE BENGHAZI ATTACKS

Benghazi, a city in Libya, was the site of a 2012 attack that hung over Obama's presidency. That year, Islamic militants attacked two US compounds in the city, resulting in the death of the US ambassador to Libya, John Christopher Stevens. This was the first time since 1988 that a US ambassador had died in a violent dispute. Investigations found that the US government had failed to both prevent and counter the attacks, and Obama's critics placed the blame on his administration.

PROTECTING THE ENVIRONMENT

Obama worked to protect the environment. His administration issued rules to stop harmful pollution from getting into the air. It formed partnerships with national and international organizations devoted to addressing climate change. For instance, in 2016, Obama signed the Paris Agreement. This agreement was adopted by many countries that wanted to fight climate change. Through the agreement, the countries promised to lower the amount of greenhouse gases they put into the air. Greenhouse gases have caused Earth to warm and have brought about climate change.

When ratifying the Paris Agreement in 2016, Obama met with world leaders such as Chinese president Xi Jinping, *center*, and United Nations secretary general Ban Ki-moon, *left*.

First Lady Michelle Obama helped organize the Reach Higher Initiative to educate students about job opportunities and the skills and education needed to reach their career goals.

MICHELLE OBAMA

Before becoming First Lady, Michelle Obama was a lawyer. When her husband became president, Michelle looked for ways to help people in the United States—especially children. In 2010, she started the Let's Move! program. This program tried to fight childhood obesity. It brought healthier foods to families and schools. It also encouraged people to exercise. During her time as First Lady, Michelle also advocated for girls around the world to receive an education.

QUICK FACTS

Birth: August 4, 1961
Wife: Michelle (LaVaughn Robinson) Obama
Number of children: Two
Age at inauguration: 47
Years served as president: 2009–2017
Supreme Court appointments: Sonia Sotomayor, Elena Kagan
Key Cabinet members:
  • Vice President: Joseph Biden

• Secretary of State: Hillary R. Clinton, John F. Kerry
• Secretary of the Treasury: Timothy F. Geithner, Jack Lew
• Secretary of Defense: Chuck Hagel, Robert M. Gates, Leon E. Panetta, Ashton B. Carter
• Attorney General: Eric H. Holder, Loretta E. Lynch

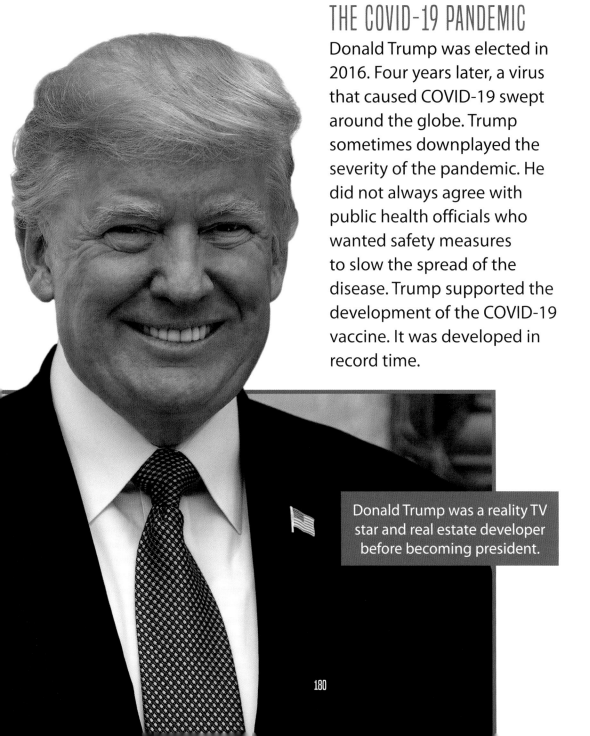

45TH
DONALD TRUMP (2017–2021)

THE COVID-19 PANDEMIC

Donald Trump was elected in 2016. Four years later, a virus that caused COVID-19 swept around the globe. Trump sometimes downplayed the severity of the pandemic. He did not always agree with public health officials who wanted safety measures to slow the spread of the disease. Trump supported the development of the COVID-19 vaccine. It was developed in record time.

Donald Trump was a reality TV star and real estate developer before becoming president.

Trump's order to create Operation Warp Speed helped the United States quickly develop a COVID-19 vaccine.

SUCCESSES IN OFFICE

People have strived to achieve peace in the Middle East for decades. In 2020, the Trump administration brought the United Arab Emirates and Bahrain together to sign the Abraham Accords. This document formalized diplomatic relations between these Arab states and Israel, which have had conflicts in the past, to bring peace and stability to the Middle East. That year, Morocco and Sudan also signed the Abraham Accords.

While in office, Trump signed the United States-Mexico-Canada Agreement. This trade agreement between the three countries helped bolster US trade and supported US workers.

In 2019, Trump created the US Space Force, which became the sixth branch of the US Military. The Space Force is responsible for military interests in space. For instance, the United States has military systems such as satellites that orbit Earth. These satellites can spot missile launches and collect intelligence data. GPS satellites also assist the military in hitting targets on Earth.

IMPEACHMENTS

In 2019, Trump encouraged the president of Ukraine to look into a potential corruption charge that involved the son of Trump's political rival, Joseph Biden. Trump's critics saw this as an abuse of power. The US House of Representatives impeached Trump, but he was acquitted by the Senate and remained in office.

In 2020, Trump lost his bid for reelection. He said the election had been stolen from him, although the US Department of Justice found no evidence of widespread fraud. Trump's words inspired anger among many of his supporters. On January 6, 2021, a crowd of them stormed the US Capitol to overturn the election. They wanted to keep Trump as president but failed to do this. The US House of Representatives impeached Trump again. They said he encouraged a rebellion against the US government. The Senate again acquitted Trump.

Many US citizens believed the January 6 breach of the US Capitol was worrisome. They viewed the action as a threat to US democracy and the peaceful transfer of presidential power.

QUICK FACTS

Birth: June 14, 1946

Wives: Ivana (Zelnickova) Trump (m. 1977–1992), Marla Maples (m. 1993–1999), Melania (Knauss) Trump (m. 2005–)

Number of children: Five

Age at inauguration: 70

Years served as president: 2017–2021

Supreme Court appointments: Neil Gorsuch, Brett Kavanaugh, Amy Coney Barrett

Key Cabinet members:
- Vice President: Mike Pence
- Secretary of State: Rex W. Tillerson, Mike Pompeo
- Secretary of the Treasury: Steven Mnuchin
- Secretary of Defense: James Mattis, Mark T. Esper
- Attorney General: Jeff Sessions, William Barr

FIGHTING THE PANDEMIC

Joseph "Joe" Biden became president in 2021 during the COVID-19 pandemic. Some state governments imposed lockdowns to stop the spread of the virus. That meant nonessential businesses had to close. This hurt the economy. People lost their jobs. They worried about losing their homes because they could not make the payments. Americans wanted to get the economy back on track. When Biden entered office, job growth was slow and unemployment was high. In Biden's first year, Congress passed the president's American Rescue Plan. That plan helped boost the economy. Employers added 6.7 million jobs to the workforce.

Joe Biden spent 36 years serving in the US Senate for the state of Delaware.

During the pandemic, Biden often wore a mask to help reduce the spread of COVID-19. He encouraged other Americans to do the same.

A STRUGGLING ECONOMY

The economy remained a challenge for Biden as he entered his second year in office. While the unemployment rate was shrinking, there were still shortages of workers in some industries. A worker shortage in manufacturing industries added to supply-chain problems. That made it hard to get some goods to consumers. At the same time, inflation was on the rise. This increased costs for goods and services and impacted people across the country. Energy prices were increasing too. In 2022, for the first time in US history, the average gas price in the nation reached more than $5 per gallon. People struggled to adjust to the high prices.

CHALLENGES AND SUCCESSES

Biden faced challenges when it came to illegal immigration. After he took office, a record number of migrants began arriving at the US-Mexico border. In May 2022 alone, 239,416 migrants trying to cross the border were arrested by US agents. Biden's critics said his opinions had encouraged people to try to get into the country. Previously, Biden had stated he would grant legal status to millions of illegal immigrants in the United States, though this idea was rejected by Congress.

As president, Trump had pulled the United States out of the Paris Agreement. After taking office, Biden rejoined this agreement. Biden's supporters praised him for this. Biden was

People trying to get into the United States through the US-Mexico border are often stopped by US authorities.

Kamala Harris was Biden's vice president. She was the first woman in US history elected to that position.

also able to get his infrastructure bill passed through Congress. This bill provided money to states to build and repair roads, railroads, and bridges in the country.

QUICK FACTS

Birth: November 20, 1942
Wives: Neilia (Hunter) Biden (m. 1966–1972), Dr. Jill (Jacobs) Biden (m. 1977–)
Number of children: Four
Age at inauguration: 78
Years served as president: 2021–
Supreme Court appointments: Ketanji Brown Jackson

Key Cabinet members:
- Vice President: Kamala Harris
- Secretary of State: Antony Blinken
- Secretary of the Treasury: Janet Yellen
- Secretary of Defense: Lloyd J. Austin III
- Attorney General: Merrick Garland

GLOSSARY

bipartisan
Describing a circumstance when two political parties work together in support of a bill or program.

cede
To give up something.

deficit
An economic state when more money has been spent than has been made.

delegate
A person sent to a convention to represent a group or a state.

desegregated
To undo the practice of separating groups of people based on race, gender, ethnicity, or other factors.

discrimination
Unfair treatment of other people, usually because of race, age, or gender.

embargo
A government order that restricts the trade of commodities or goods.

Founding Father
A leading figure who helped establish the United States of America.

impeachment
The act of charging an elected official with wrongdoing.

inflation
An increase in the price of goods and services.

interest rate
The amount charged for a person or business to borrow money.

monopoly
The condition of having exclusive control over something, such as a service or commodity.

ratified
To have given formal approval.

secede
To formally withdraw from a political union.

tariff
A set of prices, fees, duties, or taxes on imported or exported goods.

Union
During the Civil War, the Northern states led by President Abraham Lincoln.

veto
The power of a president to reject a bill passed by the legislative branch.

TO LEARN MORE

FURTHER READINGS

Bausum, Ann. *Our Country's Presidents: A Complete Encyclopedia of the U.S. Presidency, 2020 Edition*. National Geographic Kids, 2021.

Davis, Todd, and Marc Frey. *The New Big Book of U.S. Presidents*. Running Press Kids, 2021.

Parker, Philip, and Shannon Reed. *The Presidents Visual Encyclopedia*. DK, 2021.

ONLINE RESOURCES

Booklinks
NONFICTION NETWORK
FREE! ONLINE NONFICTION RESOURCES

To learn more about US presidents, please visit **abdobooklinks.com** or scan this QR code. These links are routinely monitored and updated to provide the most current information available.

INDEX

PHOTO CREDITS

Cover Photos: Victorian Traditions/Shutterstock Images, front (George Washington); Shutterstock Images, front (flag), back (presidential seal icon); Willie Pena/Shutterstock Images, front (presidential seal); Wikimedia, front (Abraham Lincoln), front (Barack Obama), front (Ronald Reagan); Jason Sponseller/Shutterstock Images, back (flag)

Interior Photos: Keith Lance/iStockphoto, 1, 55; Howard L. Sachs/Consolidated News Pictures/Archive Photos/Getty Images, 2, 167; Everett Collection/Shutterstock Images, 3, 6–7, 7, 10, 13, 18, 24, 27, 28, 32, 37, 38, 42, 47, 50–51, 52, 63, 67, 68, 72, 75, 78, 81, 82, 84, 85, 86, 88, 89, 90, 91, 95, 96, 101, 104, 105, 109, 110, 111, 113, 119, 120, 121, 130, 133, 179; iStockphoto, 4, 21, 25, 40, 45, 49, 51, 53, 56, 65; John Parrot/Stocktrek Images/Getty Images, 8; Shutterstock Images, 9, 15, 166; MPI/Archive Photos/Getty Images, 11, 61, 92; Charles Phelps Cushing/Classic Stock/Archive Photos/Getty Images, 12; Graphica Artis/Archive Photos/Getty Images, 14, 26, 74; Lana G./Shutterstock Images, 16; Orhan Cam/Shutterstock Images, 17; Bettmann/Getty Images, 19, 22, 23, 44–45, 60, 69, 102, 106, 114, 115, 117, 118, 123, 125, 129, 134, 135, 136, 138, 139, 143, 144–145, 149, 152; Heritage Art/Heritage Images/Hulton Archive/Getty Images, 20–21, 39; Jon Bilous/Shutterstock Images, 29; Universal History Archive/Universal Images Group/Getty Images, 30; Stock Montage/Archive Photos/Getty Images, 31, 97, 108, 112, 124; 3LH-Fine Art/SuperStock, 33; Heritage Art/Heritage Images/Hulton Fine Art Collection/Getty Images, 34, 36, 54, 57, 58, 62; Sepia Times/Universal Images Group/Getty Images, 35; Education Images/Universal Images Group/Getty Images, 41, 71; Ullstein Bild Dtl./ullstein bild/Getty Images, 43; Pictures from History/Universal Images Group/Getty Images, 46; Archive PL/Alamy, 48–49, ; Brady-Handy Photograph Collection/Library of Congress, 59; Kean Collection/Archive Photos/Getty Images, 64; Strobridge & Co. Lith/Library of Congress, 66; VCG Wilson/Fine Art/Corbis Historical/Getty Images, 70; Library of Congress/Hulton Archive/Getty Images, 73; Mike Stewart/AP Images, 76; Hulton Archive/Getty Images, 77; PHAS/Universal Images Group/Getty Images, 79; Apic/Hulton Archive/Getty Images, 80; Glasshouse Vintage/Universal History Archive/Education Images/Universal Images Group/Getty Images, 83; PF-usna/Alamy, 87; Historical/Corbis Historical/Getty Images, 93, 161, 163, 165; Everett Collection/SuperStock, 94; AP Images, 98–99, 107, 126, 131, 137, 140, 145, 146, 147, 151, 153, 154, 155, 159; Library of Congress/Corbis Historical/VCG/Getty Images, 99; Hulton Archive/Archive Photos/Getty Images, 100, 116, 128, 164; Archive Photos/Getty Images, 103; Photo 12/Universal Images Group/Getty Images, 122, 156; Photo Quest/Archive Photos/Getty Images, 127; Library of Congress, 132; Keystone-France/Gamma-Keystone/Getty Images, 141; Schirner/Ullstein Bild/Getty Images, 142; Bachrach/Archive Photos/Getty Images, 148; Barry Thumma/AP Images, 157; Bob Daugherty/AP Images, 158; Universal Images Group/Getty Images, 160; Greg Gibson/AP Images, 168; Jeffrey Markowitz/Sygma/Getty Images, 169; Vincent Almavy/AFP/Getty Images, 170; Joseph Sohm/Shutterstock Images, 171; Eric Draper/Library of Congress, 172; Doug Mills/AP Images, 173 (left); Seth McAllister/AFP/Getty Images, 173 (right); David J. Phillip/AP Images, 174; Jim Watson/AFP/Getty Images, 175; Pete Souza/Library of Congress, 176–177; Win McNamee/Getty Images News/Getty Images, 177; How Hwee Young/AFP/Getty Images, 178; Shealah Craighead/Library of Congress, 180; Tasos Katopodis/Getty Images News/Getty Images, 181; Sebastian Portillo/Shutterstock Images, 183; Drew Angerer/Getty Images News/Getty Images, 184; Biksu Tong/Shutterstock Images, 185; Ringo Chiu/Shutterstock Images, 186; Sheila Fitzgerald/Shutterstock Images, 187

ABDOBOOKS.COM

Published by Abdo Reference, a division of ABDO, PO Box 398166, Minneapolis, Minnesota 55439. Copyright © 2023 by Abdo Consulting Group, Inc. International copyrights reserved in all countries. No part of this book may be reproduced in any form without written permission from the publisher. Encyclopedias™ is a trademark and logo of Abdo Reference.

Printed in the United States of America, North Mankato, Minnesota.
102022
012023

THIS BOOK CONTAINS
RECYCLED MATERIALS

Editor: Alyssa Sorenson
Series Designer: Colleen McLaren

LIBRARY OF CONGRESS CONTROL NUMBER: 2022940661

PUBLISHER'S CATALOGING-IN-PUBLICATION DATA

Names: McKinney, Donna B., author.
Title: The presidents encyclopedia / by Donna B. McKinney
Description: Minneapolis, Minnesota: Abdo Publishing, 2023 | Series: United States encyclopedias | Includes online resources and index.
Identifiers: ISBN 9781098290481 (lib. bdg.) | ISBN 9781098275808 (ebook)
Subjects: LCSH: Presidents--Juvenile literature. | Presidents--United States--Juvenile literature.| United States--Officials and employees--Juvenile literature. | Encyclopedias and dictionaries--Juvenile literature.
Classification: DDC 973.099--dc23